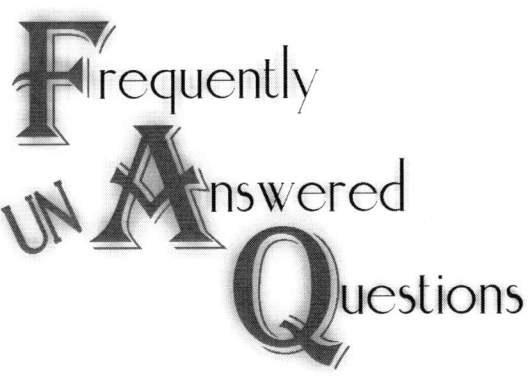

Frequently unAnswered Questions

Chaitanya Charan Das, BE COEP

VOICE
Rekindling Wisdom, Reviving Love

Vedic Oasis for Inspiration, Culture and Education (VOICE),
4, Tarapore Road
Next to Dastur Boys' School, Pune – 411 001,
Phone: (020) 26332328,
publications@voicepune.com, info@voicepune.com

ii

VOICE invites readers interested in this book to correspond at the following address:

Sales Manager:
Krishnakishore das
A-102, Bharati Vihar, Katraj, Pune – 411 046
Phone: +91-020-24306330
krishnakishoredas@gmail.com

First Printing: 16th September 2010
Second Printing: 17th February 2011

FAQ-1-150910/PLD/DJOFBSUT-Q/80-ITC-M/300-DUPLEX/XS

To,
My spiritual guides, who answered my many questions.
and
All of you, my brothers and sisters.

Introduction

> "I keep six honest serving-men,
> (They taught me all I knew);
> Their names are What and Why and When
> And How and Where and Who."

> - Rudyard Kipling

Questions and answers (QA) fascinated me since my childhood. Science, history, geography, culture, politics: whatever the field, so much could be learnt so quickly through QA with experts of those fields. Interestingly, I never thought QA applied to spirituality because I never met anyone who could answer spiritual questions logically and coherently. So, imagine my surprise and delight when, during my engineering college years, I met spiritual teachers who could answer practically every question that I could think of. These erudite young spiritual experts from an ancient non-sectarian tradition of God consciousness very kindly spent many, many long hours answering hundreds of my questions. I was further intrigued to know that the Vedic literatures from which they drew their knowledge – the Bhagavad-gita and the Srimad Bhagavatam – were themselves in the form of catechisms or questions and answers.

So inspired was I by the profound wisdom that emerged from our QA sessions that I resolved to start sharing as much of it as I could. Even today, after having lived over a dozen years as a spiritual teacher myself, I am still fascinated by QA sessions. I am still very much a student, eager to learn from my many teachers. I know I will remain a student till my last breath, always looking forward to learning through QA.

But over the years I have discovered another way to relish the joy of QA: by trying to answer carefully and succinctly the questions that come to me during my interactions with spiritual seekers. Often, even after answering a question, I find myself pondering over it, thinking of points, facts, arguments and quotes that could enrich the answer. Whenever I arrive at a more complete answer based on scripture and logic, I long to meet that questioner and provide this answer. But due to my constant travelling and interacting with hundreds of people, it is almost impossible to get back to the questioner. From the desire to resolve that predicament was born the idea of this book.

The book that you hold materialized due to another happenstance. A few years ago, the editor of the newspaper Sakaaltimes invited me to contribute an article every week to its Soul Curry column. Soon, the article became an edited rendition of the best QA interaction that I had during that week. I would sometimes slightly reframe the question to make it relevant and appealing to a broad variety of readers. Also, I would significantly edit and refine my answer so that it contained the best of all that I had learnt from my spiritual master, my many other spiritual mentors and the Vedic books of wisdom. Initially, I felt constrained by the word limit of the column, but soon condensing the answer to within 450 words became a joyful struggle. The joy came from the awareness that, by meeting the word limit without compromising on the content of the answer, I was optimizing my service to my readers. The opportunity to give my busy readers the best worth for the time they were investing in reading the articles inspired me to edit, re-edit and re-re-edit. The request of several of the regular readers of the column for a book-length compilation of those articles, along with my above-mentioned longing to offer the best answer to my questioners, led to the genesis of this book.

A few words about the structure of the book are apt here. Each article is complete in itself and so any article can be read at random. In fact, one purpose of compiling this anthology of short articles is to offer readers quick spiritual refreshment that can be availed during short breaks in their busy schedule. Some repetition of thoughts – especially in the conclusions of the articles – is inevitable in an anthology like this, but I have selected only articles with non-repetitive themes for the book. The articles within each section proceed systematically from one theme to another and so a sequential reading will help in getting optimum understanding of the subject. As an example of section structure, let's have a look at the first section "A Higher Science":

1. Articles 1 to 4 deal with common questions about God's existence,
2. Articles 5 to 7 address similar questions about the soul's existence,
3. Articles 8 and 9 talk about the recent attempts to create artificial life,
4. Articles 10 to 12 demonstrate the relevance of spirituality in an age of science
5. Articles 13 to 15 look at the interface of science and spirituality.

The other three sections are similarly structured, but I will let you discover those structures and thus avoid making this already long introduction longer.

So what you, my dear reader, are holding in your hand is a compilation of revised and refined QA articles. If these QA articles could transmit a fraction of the illumination that I received from the QA sessions with my teachers, I would consider my service to you and to my teachers a success.

Chaitanya Charan das,
Spiritual Mentor, VOICE.
Associate-Editor, Back to Godhead International Magazine

Contents

A HIGHER SCIENCE

PRACTICAL PHILOSOPHY

Toward Self-Empowerment

Vedic Insights

A Higher Science

A Higher Science

A TELESCOPE TO SEE GOD?

Question: If God exists, why can't we see him?

Answer: All of us can see God, but we need the appropriate apparatus and procedures just as we would need a telescope to see a distant celestial object.

Consider the following statement of Albert Einstein, "The deeper one penetrates into nature's secrets, the greater becomes one's respect for God." Let's try to penetrate into the secrets of one of the most astonishing natural phenomena: bird migration.

The book *Nature's IQ* written by two Hungarian ISKCON scientists, Hornyánszky Balázs and Tasi István, gives the example of the ruby-throated hummingbird (*archilochus colubris*). This bird, which weights less than three grams, is the only colibri species nesting in the eastern part of North America, yet every year it flies across the Gulf of Mexico to spend its winters in Mexico and Central America – a distance of almost 1000 kilometers – without stopping for food or rest. The flight takes twenty-five hours, and to keep aloft, the hummingbird flaps its wings seventy-five times per second, a total of more than six million continuous wing strokes. To have energy for this stupendous journey, the hummingbird stores surplus fat during the period preceding migration (it roughly doubles its weight to six grams). But how does the hummingbird know when it is time to fatten itself up?

How does it know how to find its way accurately over the 1000 km journey? The authors convincingly show how these questions have no adequate reductionist explanations. The only reasonable explanation is that God who resides in the heart of all creatures is guiding them with a part of his own infinite wisdom

So, to see God, firstly one needs to have the appropriate intellectual apparatus: a deep logical and scientific understanding of the profound order in nature along with its philosophical implications.

ISKCON scientist Dr Michael Cremo in his landmark books, *Forbidden Archaeology* and *Human Devolution,* explains systematically the severe theoretical and evidential problems with the present reductionist worldview of science. He also lucidly delineates the scientific basis for an alternative theistic worldview and gives the scientific process of mantra chanting that brings about the evolution of our consciousness. When our consciousness  has evolved sufficiently, we can free our perception from being shackled to matter. Then we can observe and experience the spiritual realm and interact with God, just as we are currently observing and experiencing the material realm and interacting with people here.

So, adopting this scientific apparatus and procedure is like enhancing our vision with a spiritual telescope to see God. Aren't atheists who refuse to try out this experiential confirmation of the God hypothesis no less fanatical than the dogmatic clergymen who refused to look through Galileo's telescope when told that they could themselves confirm the Copernican hypothesis?

଼୦

DID MAN MAKE GOD?

Question: Is the concept of God not created by man to maintain morality in human society?

Answer: Not at all.

This argument is advanced by those who imagine God to be a mere subjective conception, not an objective reality. But the fallacy of their reasoning is seen by placing their argument in a different context: is preventive medicine not created by man to maintain health in human society? Yes. But does this prove that preventive medicine doesn't exist? Obviously not. Similarly, awareness of God's existence can indeed help maintain morality in society, but this does not prove God's non-existence.

The argument that God is created by man also fails to answer the more fundamental questions: Who created man? And who created man's sense of morality? If we let the enormous scientific evidence of order, harmony and structured organization speak for itself, it unambiguously points to the existence of a super-intelligent designer. As Isaac Newton stated, "The wonderful arrangement and harmony of the cosmos would only originate in the plan of an almighty omniscient being. This is and remains my greatest comprehension."

Our sense of morality – the inner awareness of right and wrong – is almost universal. People from different cultural upbringings may disagree about what constitutes right and wrong, but nobody disagrees with the principle of there being right and wrong courses of action. Can atheists explain the origin of this sense of morality? According to them, all actions are guided by only one principle:

survival of the fittest. Then why do people risk their own survival to ensure the survival of others, as in fire accidents or swimming mishaps? And why do the rest of us consider such saviors to

be glorious? Obviously, the "survival of the fittest" notion, when applied to human morality, is not fit enough to survive. Then where does our moral sense come from? The *Bhagavad-gita* (15.15) describes that it comes from our creator, who has the original sense of morality and who is from within prompting us to make the right choices, choices conducive to our long-term inner growth and not just our immediate survival.

The Vedic scriptures also equip us to personally confirm the existence of God. They teach *bhakti* (devotion) as a scientific process that delivers experience of God, an experience so satisfying that it makes us indifferent to all other experiences. The easiest way to cultivate *bhakti* is by chanting God's holy names. Chanting has empowered millions of people all over the world to break free from bad habits like smoking, drinking and taking drugs, thus proving that they have experienced God – and that God exists.

If we too open our minds to experience God by chanting, then we can confirm for ourselves that man – and his moral sense – is created by God, not vice versa.

ॐ

WHO CREATED GOD?

Question: If God created everything, who created God?

Answer: Let's consider the answer in three different ways.

1. Once a person read a novel for the first time in his life. On coming  to know that the novel was written by an author, he asked, "Where is the author in the novel?" The above question is quite similar to that. The answer obviously is that the author is not in the novel; he created the timeline, the storyline and the characters in the novel, but he exists outside the novel. Similarly, God created time, space and everything, including all of us, who live within time and space, but he himself exists outside the fabric of time and space. So, everything that exists within time and space needs a beginning, a cause, but God who exists outside it, needs no cause, for he is the cause of time and space.

2. The Vedic literatures provide us the definition of God: *sarva karana karanam*. "He is the cause of all causes." This definition implies that, while tracing back the origin of all the things around us, the point where we stop is God. If God were to have an origin, then that origin would be God. Even according to pure logic, the source of everything cannot have a source. So this question is itself illogical as it originates in an illogical understanding of the term, God.

3. Modern science has confirmed that our universe has a beginning, that it is not eternal. Most current scientific theories propose the origin of the universe as a singularity, a point of infinite density,

infinite temperature and infinitesimal size, a point that is beyond all conceptions of space and time, a point that is mathematically indescribable and physically unrealizable. And science has no reasonable answer to the question of where this singularity came from. Thus even so-called rational science cannot avoid ascribing inconceivable (we could say "irrational") attributes to the origin of everything, but it is ascribing them to a lump of matter instead of God. So materialistic science and spirituality both require us to accept on faith their version of how the universe originated. But let's examine: which faith is more reasonable? Does a lump of matter organize itself into a building or does an intelligent person organize lumps of matter into a building? All experience points to an intelligent person. So isn't it logical that the organization, structure and harmony in the universe – the cosmic building we live in – require a Super-intelligent Person, not just a super-energetic lump of matter?

No wonder Ralph Waldo Emerson stated, "All I have seen inspires me to believe in Him for all I have not seen."

છ

IS GOD A CRUTCH?

Question: Is God not a psychological crutch for the weak-hearted?

Answer: This argument is advanced by atheists who imagine that weak-hearted people need some psychological support to face the problems of life and so have conjured a helper and protector, God.

Let's deal with this argument in three parts:

1. Does the psychological need for God disprove the existence of God?

It is true that when faced with life's problems, many people feel the need for God's protection, guidance and solace. But to claim that this need for God is all that there is to him, that he doesn't exist objectively is pathetic logic. In times of hunger, we feel the need for food. Does our need for food disprove the existence of food? Does our psychological need for relationships disprove the existence of relatives? In fact, our deep, essential needs are associated with real objects that fulfill those needs. So, the near-universal need for God that is felt by people at some time or other of their lives strongly suggests the existence of a real person, God, who fulfills that need.

2. Could atheism be a crutch for the weak-hearted?

The psychological crutch argument is a two-way sword. It could well be argued that atheists frequently indulge in wrongdoings and dread the resulting pinch of guilt and fear of future punishment.

Due to the weak-heartedness caused by their guilt and fear, they have devised the psychological crutch of atheism.

3. Are religious believers weak-hearted?

In his book *Is Religion Dangerous?* Keith Ward mentions a number of scientific studies about the relationship between religion and happiness, mental health and altruism. These studies show that religious people are neither weak-minded nor mentally ill. On the contrary, religious people are usually psychologically stronger than non-religious people and they also tend to be happier and healthier, and to live longer and be more altruistic. They tend to be less likely to suffer from hypertension, depression and criminal delinquency. 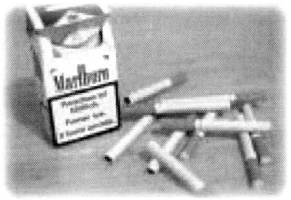 Young religious people tend to lower levels of drug and alcohol abuse, criminal delinquency and attempted suicide. So there's no scientific basis to support the atheistic claim that people are religious because they are weak-hearted. In fact, the evidence is strongly to the contrary, as confirmed by Dr Patrick Glynn in his book *God: The Evidence:* "it is difficult to find a more consistent correlative of mental health, or a better insurance against self-destructive behaviors, than a strong religious faith."

The Vedic scriptures explain that we are eternally related to God as his beloved parts. As parts, we are always dependent on God, who is the whole. By acknowledging our dependence on God, we regain our innate spiritual potency, which empowers us to grow from weak to strong and from strong to stronger.

ॐ

PROOF OF SOUL'S EXISTENCE?

Question: Is there any scientific proof for the soul's existence?

Answer: There's plenty.

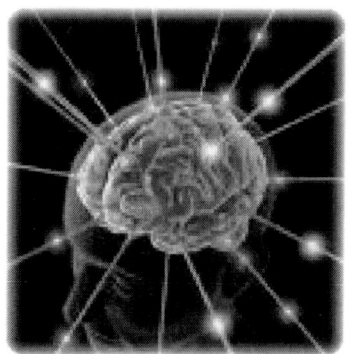

One of the most striking proofs is documented by the renowned father of modern neurosurgery, Dr Wilder Penfield, in his book *The Mystery of the Mind*. Let's consider one of his many experiments, paraphrased here without the technical jargon for easy understanding.

Dr Penfield set up a high-tech system to observe the brain activity of a subject, who was told to do simple activities like raising his hand. When he raised his arm, a certain part of the brain was activated and the subject described the event as: "I raised my arm." When he brought his arm down, that part of the brain was seen to be deactivated and the subject described the event as: "I put my arm down."

Then Dr Penfield, using state-of-the-art technology, artificially activated that part of the brain and the arm rose up. The subject described the event as: "My arm went up." Dr Penfield specifically asked: "Did you raise your arm?" The subject replied with full certainty: "I didn't raise my hand. My arm rose up by itself." When Dr Penfield deactivated the brain and the arm went down, the patient described: "My arm fell down; I did not bring it down."

This simple experiment had profound implications: in both cases, the brain was activated to raise and lower the arm. But in the second case, Dr Penfield, an external agent, was activating the brain. Who was the agent activating it in the first case? In both cases, the brain was serving as a machine to transmit the intention of an agent. In the second case, it transmitted Dr Penfield's intention. In the first case, whose intention did it  transmit? Could the mysterious agent be the soul? Dr Penfield had started his brain research with the explicit intention of disproving the existence of the soul, but after conducting experiments like the above one for forty years, he came to an unambiguous conclusion: "The brain is a computer, but it is programmed by something outside of itself."

The *Bhagavad-gita* explains what that "something outside of itself" is: the soul, or, more specifically, the consciousness, which is the intrinsic energy of the soul temporarily projected into the body. Modern science offers us strong proof for the existence of the soul. And if we want to personally experience ourselves as souls distinct from our bodies, the *Gita* offers us the higher-dimensional science of bhakti-yoga. This science, by tapping the power of divine sound, uncovers our latent spiritual consciousness, gives us direct perception of the soul and ultimately helps us reclaim our spiritual birthright to an eternal life of knowledge and bliss.

৪০

PROOF OF REINCARNATION?

Question: Is there any proof of reincarnation?

Answer: Certainly; there's lot.

But before we can understand the proof of reincarnation, we  need to understand how reincarnation takes place. The *Bhagavad-gita* explains that our current existence is three-dimensional: physical (related with the gross material body that we can see and touch), mental (related with the subtle material body centered on the mind) and spiritual (related with the soul). At the time of death, the soul, along with the subtle body, goes to the next gross body, leaving the present gross body behind. As the same subtle body carries on to the next life, aspects related to the subtle body – skills, fears and memories – are carried on from this life to the next, along with, of course, the devotional experiences associated with the soul. Whether the aspects related with the subtle body – skills, fears and memories – will be remembered in the next life or not will depend on, among other factors, the extent of impressions that have been created in the mind by the activities related to them.

Here are examples of phenomenon that persuasively point to reincarnation:

1. Precocious children who have abilities far greater than their age are a medical mystery. How does a child of five solve complex calculus problems that graduate level students struggle with? Because he has cultivated math skills in his previous life.

2. Many people with mental problems – especially phobias – that are incurable by normal psychotherapy have been cured by Dr. Brian Weiss of the Sinai Medical Research Center, USA. He traces, through hypnotically-induced past life regression, that these phobias originate in a traumatic previous-life death caused by the very object toward which one has phobia in this life. For example, he found that several patients having hydrophobia had died due to drowning in a previous life. When the patients understand the cause of the phobia, then their phobia disappears or at least decreases dramatically. Those who don't consider reincarnation real have no explanation for the real healing that has taken place.

3. Numerous cases of past-life memories are documented by rigorous researchers like Dr. Ian Stevenson in his books, especially *Where Reincarnation and Biology Intersect*. Dr Stevenson's research quality was acknowledged in the prestigious *Journal of the American Medical Association*: "[Dr Stevenson had] painstakingly and unemotionally collected a detailed series of cases in which the evidence for reincarnation is difficult to understand on any other grounds....He has placed on record a large amount of data that cannot be ignored."

Considering these multiple proofs, no wonder author Collin Watson asserted, "The sheer volume of evidence for survival after death is so immense, that to ignore it is like standing at the foot of Mt. Everest and insisting that you cannot see the mountain."

LET'S BECOME SPIRITUAL DETECTIVES

Question: We need food for energy. So isn't the claim that the soul is the source of energy in the body disproved by everyday experience?

Answer: No.

In the *Bhagavad-gita* (18.34) Lord Krishna explains the relationship between the soul and the body with an insightful analogy: "As the sun illuminates the universe, so does the soul illuminate the body by consciousness." The sun's illumination is necessary for  vegetation to grow on the earth, as is the supply of water. For the growth of the vegetation, the sunlight is the remote cause and the water, the immediate cause. An uninformed gardener may think that the plant needs water alone, because that is what he or she has to provide. But a wise gardener knows that sunlight plays an equally indispensable role. Similarly, for bodily energy, food is the immediate cause and the soul, the remote cause. An uninformed person may think that the body needs food alone, because that is what he or she has to provide. But a wise person knows that food alone is not enough for energy; food cannot energize a dead person.

Nor can food – or the matter that constitutes it – account for the essential characteristic of life, consciousness: the ability to be aware of and to experience our surroundings, and to respond with thoughts, feelings, intentions and actions. For example, a sweet is made of matter and so is the tongue. The sweet does not experience itself as delicious. But when we place the sweet on our tongue, we experience it as delicious. Who is experiencing that taste? The tongue? Or some part of the brain? But both the tongue and the brain are essentially made of the same material components as the sweet: molecules, atoms, subatomic particles, quantum wave patterns. Nothing in these material components even remotely resembles consciousness. Modern science has utterly failed to even theoretically explain how matter can experience matter, leave alone experimentally demonstrate it. That's why in the book, *Biology Today*, Nobel Laureate chemist Albert Szent-Gyorgyi admitted, "In my search for the secret of life, I ended up with atoms and electrons, which have no life at all. Somewhere along the line, life ran out through my fingers. So, in my old age, I am now retracing my steps...."

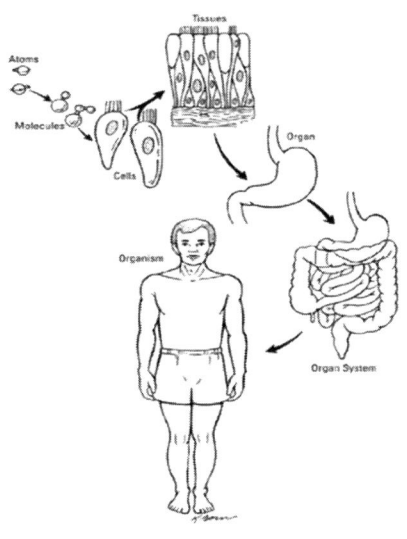

Why should we too have to retrace our steps in old age? Let us instead be bold and adventurous enough to become spiritual detectives. If we investigate the mystery of life by the process of philosophical contemplation and devotional meditation outlined in the *Gita*, all one of us can experientially verify our real identities as souls.

80

ARTIFICIAL LIFE?

Question: What is the Vedic comment on recent news report that the genome pioneer Craig Venter has created artificial life?

Answer: Let's see what Venter actually did:

1. Determined the sequence of the DNA in one of the world's simplest bacteria,

2. Synthesized a copy of that DNA from components sold by a biological supply company,

3. Replaced the natural DNA in a living bacterial cell with this synthetic DNA.

Now we need to remember that DNA is not life. It is simply a sequence of biological codes storing the instructions for building proteins. As Oxford biologist Richard Dawkins stated, "The machine code of the genes is uncannily computer-like."

So, speaking analogically, Venter has certainly not created the complete computer; he has just replaced one chip with another in a pre-existing computer. That's why Caltech biologist and Nobel laureate David Baltimore stated that Venter has "overplayed the importance" of his results; he "has not created life, only mimicked it."

What if scientists someday use the biochemical components to create the entire cell? Would that amount to creating life? No, because that would just be like making the computer, not the person who would use the computer. Although reductionist scientists would have us believe that there is no such "person" and that life is just a product of bio-chemicals, living systems behave in ways fundamentally and inexplicably different from nonliving objects. Nonliving objects are created, deteriorate over time and eventually meet with destruction. Living systems exhibits three additional features: maintenance, growth and reproduction. A living human hand, if cut, can clot and heal itself; the most state-of-the-art artificial hand, if cut, cannot clot or heal itself. The simplest unicellular organism can grow; the most sophisticated computer cannot. The most primitive 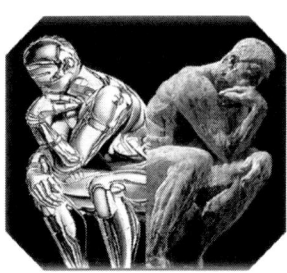 living systems can reproduce; even the most advanced robots can't.

No wonder Boston University bioengineer James Collins candidly admitted the scientific ground reality: "Scientists don't know enough about biology to create life."

What do scientists not know about life? What gives living systems their remarkable properties of maintenance, growth and reproduction? The soul, which the *Bhagavad-gita* explains, is the source of life. The soul is eternal and can never be created. The *Gita* (13.33-34) also points out that the soul remains distinct from the body it animates, as does sunlight illuminating the universe or air pervading space. So, when a part of the body is changed, the soul remains unchanged, just as when a component in a computer is changed, the computer-user remains unchanged. Thus, in Venter's experiment, the soul animating the bacteria remained unchanged when the DNA within that bacteria was changed.

To summarize, Venter's attempt at creating artificial life is a failure – both in practice (he did not create life) and in principle (the soul, the actual source of life, can never be created).

৪০

IMITATE GOD, INVITE DISASTER

Question: What are the implications of the recent attempts to create artificial life?

Answer: The attempt to create artificial life is essentially an attempt by man to imitate God. The history of science shows that, when man "plays God", what is initially hailed as a breakthrough eventually causes a breakdown.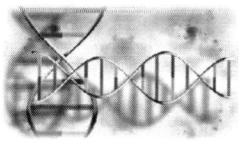

In new fields of research, scientists almost invariably promise beneficial, often sensational, future results. However, the past track record of such promises shows counterproductive, often devastating, consequences. For example, genetically-modified (GM) food was advertised as the solution to world hunger, but it ended up causing hunger-deaths of hundreds of farmers in Maharashtra, India. These farmers were captivated by promises of pest-resistant seeds and high yields, but when the pests developed resistance to the seeds, the yields failed utterly. Moreover, as the GM seeds are designed to not give seeds for the next sowing, the farmers had no chance of a yield in the next season either. Afflicted by poverty, hunger and hopelessness, multitudes of them committed suicide. Alarmed by the possible adverse consequences of GM food, the European Union has outright banned their use and concerned NGOs worldwide are striving for similar curbs.

What are the possible dangers in "artificial life" research? Genome manipulation of the kind done by Dr Venter can lead to the development of medicine-resistant variants of disease-producing microbes, which could trigger a pandemic. The genome Dr. Venter synthesized was copied from a natural bacterium that infects goats. Before copying the DNA, he claims to have excised fourteen genes likely to be pathogenic, so that the new bacterium, even if it escaped, would be unlikely to cause goats harm. But such measures may not be incorporated in future similar researches – either unintentionally or intentionally. Will we then see headlines of artificial deaths – deaths caused by attempts at artificial life – in the papers? While some may consider such a scenario unlikely and unduly pessimistic, it is certainly a possibility. And perhaps contemplation on the worst-case possibility is necessary to prevent it from becoming a reality.

On a positive note, the "artificial life" news, by bringing to the forefront the age-old question of what life actually is, may prompt some soul-searching – at least figuratively and maybe even literally. For such soul-searching, the *Bhagavad-gita* can act as a reliable, time-tested guidebook of higher dimensional science. If the energy spent on creating artificial life were directed to cultivating spiritual knowledge and practice as outlined in the *Gita*, humanity would take quantum leaps in its understanding of life. The scientific establishment may or may not do this, but each of us individually can. If we choose to become courageous soul-searchers, we will no longer be taken in by overhyped reports about artificial life, for we will be constantly experiencing and relishing the meaning of real life.

ISN'T THAT UNSCIENTIFIC ?

Question: When I talk about God, soul, rebirth, people often question: why discuss such unscientific things in this modern age of science?

Answer: Their question originates not from their scientific thinking, but from their belief in scientism, the peculiar school of thought that places around science a halo of "omniscience."

The reputed physicist Fritjof Capra in his well-known book "The Tao of Physics" explains how scientific knowledge is like a map. Just as a map helps in navigating the mapped territory, science helps in manipulating the physical world. However, a map, no matter how exhaustive, is neither the territory, nor a complete description of the territory. Similarly, scientific knowledge, no matter how exhaustive, is neither the reality, nor a complete description of the reality. If the map helps us to precisely reach a particular house in a city, where we meet the owner of the house, will we decide that the owner of the house is non-existent and imaginary because he is not shown in our map? Obviously not. Similarly, scientific knowledge may efficiently guide us in our exploration of the physical world, but when we encounter essential features of our world that are not found in the world of science – emotions, consciousness, free will, the quest for meaning and purpose, should we reject these features as unscientific and so unreal? Obviously not. Former US President Theodore Roosevelt warned eloquently about the consequences of scientism: "There is superstition in science quite as much as there is superstition in theology, and it

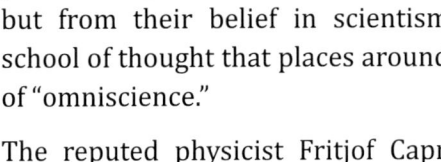

is all the more dangerous because those suffering from it are profoundly convinced that they are freeing themselves from all superstition. No grotesque repulsiveness of medieval superstition, even as it survived into nineteenth-century Spain and Naples, could be much more intolerant, much more destructive of all that is fine in morality, in the spiritual sense, and indeed in civilization itself, than that hard dogmatic materialism  of today which often not merely calls itself scientific but arrogates to itself the sole right to use the term. If these pretensions affected only scientific men themselves, it would be a matter of small moment, but unfortunately they tend gradually to affect the whole people, and to establish a very dangerous standard of private and public conduct in the public mind."

In his remarkable book *Mechanistic and Non-Mechanistic Science*, Cornell-educated scientist Dr Richard L Thompson explains how the path of *Bhakti-yoga* explained in the *Bhagavad-gita* constitutes a higher-dimensional science that incorporates God, soul and rebirth, and coherently explains the essential features of life that modern science can't explain. Most importantly, the path of *bhakti-yoga* offers each one of us the opportunity to experientially verify its truths. Thus, *bhakti-yoga* incorporates both a theoretical and an experimental sense and so is entirely scientific.

ॐ

IS FACTUAL NOT ACTUAL?

Question: Why should we bother about some other world that spiritualists often talk about? Shouldn't our actual life be based on the factual world – the world that we see around us?

Answer: The word "factual" comes from the Latin *facio*, "to make or do." Thus a fact is what has been made or done. It is a product  of the work of our senses—our seeing, hearing, touching, smelling and tasting. ISKCON scholar Suhotra Swami explains in his remarkable book, *Dimensions of Good and Evil*:

"Factual knowledge can only be knowledge of the past. When we look up at the night sky, we do not see the stars as they *are* but as they *were*. It takes time for their light to reach our eyes. According to modern cosmology, the light of many of the stars we see now may be several thousand years old. Some of them may have exploded centuries ago...The 'factual' sun that brightens our eyes is always eight minutes in the past. No one on earth has ever seen the 'actual' sun. A slight time lag divides us from even the nearest objects of our perception. This 'factual' world of human sensory experience is the phenomenal world—a world that has already changed by the time we know it. Thus the phenomenal world, the world of facts, is a world of secondary, dead information. The world that is, the primary living reality, we never know. Facts, far from being 'the whole truth', are just signals conveyed by the network of our senses."

Science can only explain the factual world, the world of the senses, whereas the actual world, the world of life, remains forever beyond the reach of science. That's why factual science is silent about the fundamental questions of existence – origin, value and purpose. And yet

knowledge of these directs our actual lives consciously and subconsciously.

The claim that science can explain all of reality, that the factual world is the actual world, is pseudoscientific and is called scientism. From the viewpoint of the *Bhagavad-gita* (18.22), scientism is knowledge in the mode of ignorance: "That knowledge by which one is attached to one kind of work as the all in all, without knowledge of the truth, and which is very meager, is said to be in the mode of ignorance." Factual knowledge makes us attached to one kind of work: material progress. It is 'knowledge in ignorance' because it increases our knowledge of the factual world, while keeping us in ignorance of the actual world.

Because we mistakenly call this dead world as "factual", spiritualists remind us of the actual world of life and love where we originally belong and where we need to return to attain the immortality and ecstasy that is our destiny.

ॐ

A Fresh Worldview

Question: Does spirituality provide anything that science cannot provide?

Answer: Yes. Spirituality provides us a fresh worldview with  purpose and meaning that is missing in the atheism which is currently dominating modern science.

"If you don't know where you are going, any road will take you there," sang Beatle George Harrison in one his popular songs. The life's journey of most modern people is often characterized by ultra-high speed and ultra-low clarity of purpose. This peculiar, even dangerous, combination is like a car-driver going superfast without knowing his destination.

Our impressive progress in technology is like providing the car-driver a faster car and a smoother expressway. Most modern people delight in driving as fast as they can, as luxuriously as they can and as long as they can. They are almost fanatical in claiming that anyone who doesn't "progress" their way is primitive, regressive and unscientific.

But why does their "progress" make them addicted to sleeping pills, anti-depressant medicines, even cigarettes, liquor, drugs? Why has their "progress" brought our world on the brink of ecological breakdown?

Insightful thinkers have already seen through the façade of "progress". Nobel Laureate physicist Erwin Schrodinger pointed

out, "I am very astonished that the
scientific picture of the real world
around me is very deficient. It gives
a lot of factual information, puts all
our experience in a magnificently
consistent order, but it is ghastly
silent about all and sundry that is
really near to our heart, that really
matters to us. It cannot tell us a word about red and blue, bitter
and sweet, physical pain and physical delight; it knows nothing of
beautiful and ugly, good or bad, God and eternity. Science sometimes
pretends to answer questions in these domains, but the answers are
very often so silly that we are not inclined to take them seriously."
Martin Luther King, Jr, stated, "The means by which we live have
outdistanced the ends for which we live. Our scientific power has
outrun our spiritual power. We have guided missiles and misguided
men."

To help us guide men, the Vedic texts offer a delightfully different
understanding of progress. Real progress comes not by finding
newer ways to manipulate matter, but by finding ways to realize the
spiritual essence of life. Spiritual realization makes us aware that we
are not destructible lumps of matter, but are indestructible sparks
of consciousness; that we are not lonely survivors in an impersonal,
cold cosmos, but are beloved children of a benevolent almighty in
a purposeful cosmos; that we are not doomed to mortality, but
are destined for immortality. By thus liberating us from the bleak
worldview of scientific atheism, spirituality brings clarity, purpose,
meaning, joy and love into our lives.

ℰↄ

CAN SCIENCE DISCOVER SPIRITUALITY?

Question: Can science by its future progress discover spiritual truths?

Answer: Yes and no.

The spiritual philosophy, explained in the *Bhagavad-gita* and other Vedic texts, is a science in its own right, for it is systematic, coherent, verifiable and repeatable – all characteristics of any good scientific theory. Unfortunately, many modern scientists define science as the study of matter alone, thus rejecting spiritual truths as "unscientific" right from the beginning without any proof whatsoever. This a priori restriction of the scope of science is evident from

geneticist Richard Lewontin's remark: "We take the side of science in spite of the patent absurdity of some of its constructs, in spite of its failure to fulfill many of its extravagant promises of health and life, in spite of the tolerance of the scientific community for unsubstantiated just-so stories because we cannot allow a Divine Foot in the door."

Such dogmatic rejection of a Divine Foot militates against the scientific spirit of free enquiry. As stated by pioneering atomic physicist Robert Oppenheimer, "[In science] there must be no barriers for freedom of inquiry. There is no place for dogma in science." Only after science breaks free from its anti-spiritual dogma can it start discovering spiritual truths. In fact, already a good number of scientists have individually shaken off the dogma and have come up with convincing evidences for the existence of God and the soul.

Still, science will at best discover only preliminary spiritual truths, not advanced. Here's why. Every field of knowledge has its own distinctive methods. To gain advanced knowledge of that field without adopting its methods is often impossible. To illustrate, let's consider different scientific instruments of increasing complexity:

1. We can measure our bodily weight quickly using a weighing machine. However, to measure the weight without using the machine, we have to adopt the cumbersome process of standing on one side of a weighing scale and stacking one kg weights on the other side until the two sides balance.

2. We can measure the distance from the earth of a particular star in a distant galaxy with a telescope. However, to measure that distance without using the telescope, we have to adopt the expensive and impractical process of boarding a spacecraft and flying until there while keeping an eye on the distance meter – assuming of course that we stay alive until then.

3. We can measure the speed of a fundamental particle using a particle accelerator. However, if we wish to measure that speed without the accelerator, it's impossible.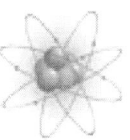

Just as science has its distinctive methodology, so does spirituality. So, scientific methodology can discover basic spiritual principles like the existence of soul and God. However, only spiritual methods like mantra meditation will enable us to experientially verify advanced spiritual principles like the identity and the personality of God.

ॐ

AREN'T YAJNAS A WASTE OF MONEY?

Question: Aren't *yajnas* (fire sacrifices) in which grains and ghee are poured into fire to be reduced to ashes a foolish waste of money?

Answer: They will appear to be a waste only as long as we are uninformed.

The Vedic texts that talk about *yajnas* assert that, just as while living in a country the citizens are duty-bound to pay taxes for the utilities provided by the national government, similarly, while living in the universe, we are expected to pay cosmic taxes for the utilities provided through nature by the cosmic government headed by God. The utilities of food, water, air, lumber, rocks, metals, jewels, oil and so forth lead to a staggering "bill to nature" for $16 trillion to $54 trillion US dollars per annum, as described in *Nature*, 15 May, 1997.

The medium of economic exchange is known to vary greatly in accordance with the prevailing socio-cultural setting. For example, if an ancient from the Vedic age is transported through time into our society, he will be aghast to see the amount of value we ascribe to the pieces of paper that we call currency notes. Just as our medium of exchange – currency notes – is unintelligible to an ancient, the Vedic medium of intra-universal exchange – sanctified fire and sound – is incomprehensible to us. An intelligent person focuses not on the medium of exchange, but the principle. We moderns give valuable things – our time and energy – to get money, and we get important things – the necessities of life – by giving money. Similarly, Vedic followers offer oblations into the sacred fire to satisfy the Cosmic Controller and in return receive profusely all the gifts of nature.

The proof of the pudding is in the eating; the proof of the authenticity of the *yajnas* is in the resulting prosperity. The prosperity of ancient India is well-known, as described both in the Vedic literatures themselves such as the Shrimad Bhagavatam as well as by many historians including A L Basham in his *The Wonder That Was India*. Indeed, the present world's most prosperous nation, USA, was discovered when explorers were searching  for new navigational routes to tap the prosperity of India! The principle of cosmic governance is also negatively evident through the present erratic supply of natural resources due to our non-remittance of our cosmic tax.

Of course, in the present age, *yajnas* are not practical due to the prohibitive costs of the required oblations as well as due to non-availability of competent priests to precisely chant the intricate mantras. Therefore, the Vedic texts recommend a method more pragmatic than fire sacrifices: sonic technology activated through mantra chanting. But the principle remains the same: harmonization with the cosmic state for sustainable prosperity. Applying this principle is by no means a waste of money; rather neglect of this principle will reduce our earth to a wasteland, as is increasingly happening nowadays.

(For a detailed answer to this question, please refer to the article "Artificial Rains" in the author's book *Science and Spirituality*)

ॐ

SYNTHESIS OF SCIENCE AND SPIRITUALITY

Question: Thinkers all over the world are striving to synthesize science and spirituality. What can the Indian wisdom-tradition contribute to this attempted synthesis?

Answer: India is renowned globally as the land of profound and peerless spiritual wisdom. Here are a few quotes of eminent Western thinkers:

1. "Whenever I have read any part of the Vedas, I have felt that some unearthly and unknown light illuminated me. In the great teaching of the Vedas, there is no touch of sectarianism. It is of all ages, climbs, and nationalities and is the royal road for the attainment of the Great Knowledge" -American Thinker Henry David Thoreau

2. "The marvel of the *Bhagavad-gita* is its truly beautiful revelation of life's wisdom which enables philosophy to blossom into religion" - Nobel Lauerate Author Hermann Hesse

Lesser known are the contributions of Vedic India to the field of science. Here are a few quotes from famous Western scientists acknowledging the scientific glory of Vedic India:

1. "We owe a lot to the Indians, who taught us how to count, without which no worthwhile scientific discovery could have been made." - Nobel Laureate Physicist Albert Einstein

2. "It is India that gave us the ingenious method of expressing all numbers by ten symbols, each receiving a value of position as well as an absolute value, a profound and important

idea which appears so simple to us now that we ignore its true merit. But its very simplicity, the great ease which it has lent to all computations, puts our arithmetic in the first rank of useful inventions, and we shall appreciate the grandeur of this achievement the more when we remember that it escaped the genius of Archimedes and Apollonius, two of the greatest men produced by antiquity." - French Mathematician Pierre Laplace

Not only does the Vedic wisdom-tradition present profound, detailed knowledge about the spiritual realm, but it also delineates systematic, time-tested and unique techniques and technologies to experience that non-material realm which is otherwise out of the reach of Western science. Thus, the Vedic tradition offers a well-developed science of consciousness study and transformation, a science that that has no parallels in any wisdom-tradition. The potential of Vedic wisdom to bridge the yawning chasm that separates science and spirituality today is expressed by many leading thinkers, among whom is the world's youngest Noble Laureate scientist: "The Vedanta and the Sankhya hold the key to the laws of mind and thought process which are co-related to the Quantum Field, i.e. the operation and distribution of particles at atomic and molecular levels." - Nobel Laureate Physicist Brian David Josephson

Indeed, by uniting reason and faith in a higher-dimensional paradigm, Vedic-wisdom can heal the wound that has torn the human brain and the human heart far apart, and thus usher a new era of integrated, holistic development in world history.

৪১

Practical Philosophy

WHY TO APPROACH GOD?

Question: Most people pray to God only to get their own desires fulfilled. Does such self-serving worship please God?

Answer: God is pleased just by our approaching him, irrespective of our motivation. But the more selfless our motive, the more God is pleased. The motives with which people approach God can be categorized into four major levels:

1. **Fear:** Some people fear, "If I disobey God, then He may punish me for my wrongdoings. So better let me go to His temple and pacify Him by my worship." This sort of worship is certainly better than atheism, but it is based on a very negative conception of God as a stern judge, a cosmic punisher.

2. **Desire:** Some people reason, "There are so many things I want; if I pray to God, perhaps He will give them to me." Here the conception of God is more positive, as a potent desire-fulfiller. Still the relationship with God is highly utilitarian based on give-and-take rather than love. Srila Prabhupada, the founder-acharya of ISKCON, would say that if we go to God to ask for bread, then that shows our love for bread, not our love for God.

3. **Duty:** Some people reason, "God has already given me so much: life, body, health, food, clothing, shelter. It is my duty to go periodically to His temple and thank Him." Here the relationship is somewhat steady, being based on gratitude for what has already been given and not on greed for what one wants to receive. Still, over time, duty can become a burden. Moreover, the focus in this level is still on what God has done for me, not on God Himself.

4. **Love:** This is the purest level of approaching God, where a devotee feels, "My dear Lord, you are the supreme object of my love; I have loved so many things and people, but it was all in vain. Now I simply want to love you and to be loved by you eternally. Just as a parent takes care of the child without the child having to ask his parents, similarly, I know that you will take care of me and so I will not ask you for anything material. I will accept whatever is your plan for me and keep serving you no matter what happens in my life." It is only this pure love that can satisfy our hearts fully, for love is the innermost need of our hearts.

The real purpose of coming to God is not to have our desires *fulfilled*, but to have our desires *purified* so that we can offer pure love to God, and relish his unlimited love in return. So, irrespective of our present level, all of us can aspire to rise to the level of pure love. And that noble aspiration can be swiftly achieved by associating with those devotees who love God purely.

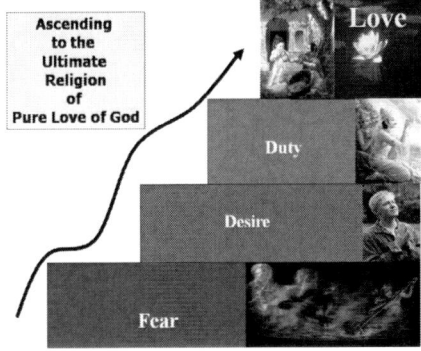

HOW TO CHOOSE THE RIGHT PATH?

Question: Among the many spiritual paths, how can we know the right path?

Answer: Let's first understand the criterion to categorize and evaluate various paths. Then the right path will become self-evident.

Various religious paths can be placed into three basic categories:

1. **Exclusivism:** Followers of exclusivist paths claim that their  way is the only exclusive way to God. They further claim that all those who don't accept their path are destined to go to hell – forever. Religious exclusivism sometimes degenerates into fundamentalist violence. This further puts off intelligent people, who are already skeptical of the claim to exclusivism. After all, if God is unlimited, why should the path to him be limited? Why should one particular religion have monopoly on the path to him?

2. **Pluralism:** Pluralism is the notion that there are many paths to God. Nowadays, this notion is sometimes expanded to say that there are as many paths to God as there are people. While this notion seems to promote religious tolerance, it often breeds spiritual impotence. A religion can be compared to a university meant to train students in knowledge and love of God. The claim to exclusivism is like the claim of that one's own medical college is the only college that can produce doctors. This is obviously a fanatical and fallacious claim. However, the claim to pluralism is like the even more fallacious claim that every building everywhere is a medical college.

3. **Inclusivism:** Inclusivism explains that there are not many paths, but basically one path that includes many levels. The levels on the path correspond to the progressively higher motives with which people approach God: fear, desire, duty and love. (Please see the previous article, "Why to approach God?")

A medical college's level can be assessed by observing the caliber of its graduates and the progress of its students toward that caliber. Similarly, the level of a religious path can be assessed by observing the caliber of its mature practitioners and the progress of its budding practitioners toward that caliber.

What caliber should we look for among mature practitioners of a spiritual path?

1. Systematic, profound knowledge of God that answers all the fundamental questions of life and establishes God as the essence and goal of existence.

2. Deep inner love for God that expresses itself by:

   a. Constant longing to worship God, chant his holy names, and relish his message of love.

   b. Care and concern for all living beings – humans and nonhumans – seeing them all as family members in God's universal family.

   c. Detachment from godless, materialistic indulgences like illicit sex and intoxication.

When we see these characteristics in the practitioners of a path, we can confidently infer that path to be the right path.

ॐ

IS KARMA RELEVANT?

Question: Do philosophical concepts like karma have any practical relevance in today's world?

Answer: Certainly. Let's see how.

Imagine a city with an entrance notice: "Welcome. There is no police force in this city; please follow the laws." How many people will follow the laws? Very few, if any.

Today's world has become like that no-police city. The law enforcement system is known to be weak and corrupt. Consequently, people think, "If I am just clever enough, influential enough or cunning enough, then I can do whatever I want and I can get away with it." Moreover, due to the prevailing godless educational system, most people no longer understand that they are accountable to God for their actions. That's why more and more people are becoming immoral and even criminal, as is seen from the following statistics:

1. In India, as per the National Crime Records Bureau, the incidences of crime since the early days of independence has gone up by more than 5 times.

2. According to the FBI, Uniform Crimes Report, the United States Crime Index Rates Per 100,000 inhabitants have increased twice from 1,887.2 in 1960 to 3,667.0 in 2008.

So, if we want people to return to morality, we need to educate them the divine law of karma, which holds them accountable for all of their actions. As is rightly said, fear of God is the beginning of wisdom, just like for a child, fear of the parent is generally the main impetus for study. How many of us have been chastised by  our parents and forced to study? Almost everyone, sometime or the other. At that time, we didn't find it pleasant, but later on we appreciate our parents for what they did. Similarly, for most people, fear is an essential, even indispensable, impetus for duty.

That's why, if there is no proper understanding of the law of karma and the fear of the karmic reactions, most people will have no impetus to live with moral integrity.

Of course, fear of God is only the beginning of wisdom; love of God is the culmination. When love for God activates our innate ethical and spiritual value system, based on the understanding that God is our greatest well wisher, then we willingly desist from immoral behavior and persist in moral behavior. But obviously, we cannot attain the culmination of wisdom without even beginning the journey. Hence, karmic knowledge has to be the basis of morality and so is supremely relevant in today's world.

૪૦

WHY NATURAL CALAMITIES?

Question: Why are we undergoing so many natural calamities like swine flu, droughts, floods, cyclones, earthquakes, hurricanes etc?

Answer: These calamities raise a fundamental question: is the anger of nature chaotic, hitting us as helpless victims? Or is there a pattern underlying this apparent madness?

According to the Vedic scriptures, all forms of sufferings are results of our own karma, our own choices of right or wrong actions. We may wonder: what wrong choices have we made to warrant so many natural calamities as reactions? Those wrong choices are primarily animal slaughter and abortion. These two activities, though rampant in our society, are declared monstrously criminal in the cosmic penal system. Why? From God's viewpoint, these two activities are brutal; His more powerful children – humans – are ruthlessly and systematically slaughtering His weaker children – animals and infants. And the main reason for this ghastly massacre is often the selfish hedonistic desire for the enjoyment of the tongue and the genitals. Especially despicable is the slaughter of cows. The cow is like our mother because she nourishes us with her milk. And we "scientifically advanced, cultured moderns" erect factories of

death to murder our bovine mothers. Not only that, nowadays human mothers, who according to poets are supposed to be "the embodiments of selfless love", murder their own children without letting them see the light of the day.

The Bhagavad-gita (4.17) declares that the system of karma is too complex for us to discover a one-to-one correspondence between action and reaction. Nonetheless, we can discern overall patterns that confirm karmic correlations. The last century – especially the second part – witnessed an unparalleled increase in animal slaughter and abortion due to the spread of factory farming and the legalization of abortion. During this period, natural calamities have also increased enormously. For example, according to the International Society for Disaster Reduction (ISDR), there were three times as many great

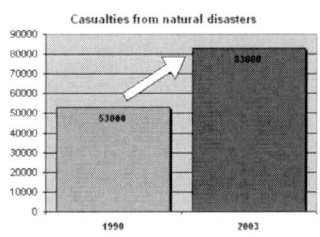

Casualties from natural disasters

natural disasters in the 1990s as in the 1960s, while disaster costs increased more than nine-fold in the same period.

Of course, not all the people killed in natural disasters may have necessarily committed animal slaughter or abortion; they succumbed to their own specific bad karma, whatever it may have been. Such disasters are examples of mass karma, during which, in addition to every individual suffering his or her own karmic reaction, the mass of people living in predominantly sinful areas undergo a shared reaction for their common misdeeds.

Thus, the overall pattern in nature's response is not difficult to see. Isn't it time for us to learn the lesson and scrupulously avoid bad karma by giving up illicit sex and meat eating, which are the root causes of abortion and animal slaughter?

(For a detailed answer to this question, please refer to the article "Natural Calamities - Why? What to do?" in the author's book *Science and Spirituality*)

৪০

CAN SPIRITUALITY END STARVATION?

Question: Can spirituality solve the real problems of the world like starvation?

Answer: Why not?

Let's analyze the root cause and the real solution of starvation.

Self-restraint: Many, if not most, of the people who starve today would be able to earn sufficiently to feed themselves and their families if only they were not addicted to self-destructive indulgences. So their starvation problem cannot be sustainably solved without freeing them from their addictions. How can they be freed from their addictions? The exhaustively-researched Oxford publication, entitled *Handbook of Religion and Health*, documents that adopting religious principles helps addicts to free themselves and also that the religiously committed are less likely to succumb to bad habits.

Compassion: The world is plagued not by a shortage of food, but by a shortage of compassion. Hundreds of tons of food is either thrown 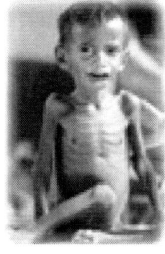 into the ocean or allowed to rot in the warehouses due to the vested interests of the powers-that-be. Frances Moore Lappé points out in her well-researched book on African famines, *Food First*, that the famines were caused or worsened because much of the best land was being misused for production of cash export crops.

How can we increase compassion and decrease greed among people? By imparting them a spiritual vision of life. When a wealthy person is God-conscious, his compassion is not restricted to an occasional act of charity; rather his whole life becomes dedicated to helping the deprived in every possible way – materially and spiritually. When the head of state is spiritually enlightened, he cares for all the citizens like his own children – not due to political expediency, but due to spiritual love. He creates the necessary socio-economic structures to provide proper gainful employment for all of them in normal situations and adequate relief during emergencies.

Henry David Thoreau pointed out, "For every thousand hacking at the leaves of evil, there is one striking at its root." Striking at the root of starvation means promoting spiritual well being both among the have-nots so that they don't dissipate their scarce resources in self-destructive indulgences and among the haves so that they don't squander their abundant resources in revelry.

The easiest and best way of promoting spiritual well being is by empowering people to understand and experience the inner satisfaction that comes from studying philosophical masterpieces like the Bhagavad-gita and by chanting the holy names of God like the Hare Krishna mahamantra. Thus, propagation of pure spiritual education and culture, as is done by ISKCON, strikes at the root cause of all suffering – including starvation.

(For a detailed answer to this question, please refer to the article "The Complete Social Service" in the author's book *Science and Spirituality*)

౪

OUR INBUILT SECURITY SYSTEM

Question: Nowadays some people advise that feelings of guilt are just primitive cultural hangovers that stop us from enjoying life fully. Is guilt harmful?

Answer: Those who give such advice are harmful.

We feel a sense of guilt whenever we act against our conscience. Our conscience – the internal voice that inspires us to do good and to avoid bad – is a great gift from God. Let's see how.

When we feel feverish, that feeling helps us know that dangerous germs are overcoming our immune system. Similarly, when we feel guilty, that feeling helps us know that self-defeating desires are overcoming our intelligence. If the fever is neglected or suppressed, then the germs may cause a complete health breakdown. Similarly, if the guilt is neglected or suppressed, then the self-defeating desires may cause a complete emotional and physical breakdown.

 For example, in the current internet age, even small children have easy, unguarded access to sexually explicit images. Looking at obscene images may be initially pleasurable, but it soon gives rise to dangerous drives that may lead to abuse of one's own and others' bodies, as also to infection by deadly diseases. When children are mis-educated to neglect the guilt – the pinch of conscience – they feel on doing wrong things, these poor children become stripped of their inbuilt defense systems and soon become overpowered by devastating habits.

Of course, guilt can make people feel worthless and helpless – and

indeed guilt is used by some fire and brimstone
fundamentalists to scare people into conforming
to their own notions of religion. But such self-
seeking misuse of guilt by some people shouldn't
blind us to its indispensable use. Guilt – and the
conscience that produces it – is ultimately meant
to connect us with the universal principles that
govern all human behavior and interactions. These principles,
as explained in the God-given scriptures like the Bhagavad-gita,
elevate our conscience from being culturally-determined to being
divinely-determined. Then we can discriminate right from wrong
based on not just our socio-cultural values but on time-tested
universal principles.

When our conscience is thus alert, our guilt not
only saves us from the suffering coming from
self-damaging choices, but also points us to
the happiness coming from self-strengthening
choices. For example, a person with a healthy
conscience will avoid visually exploiting other people's bodies and
feeling guilty and dissatisfied thereafter, but will instead visually
feast on the all-attractive form of God manifested as the Deity and
feel purified and satisfied. Similarly, in all our quests for happiness,
our guilt and conscience can redirect us from temporary, unfulfilling
surrogates to eternal, supremely fulfilling originals.

Therefore, instead of trying to get rid of the feeling of guilt, let's get
rid of the actions that cause that feeling.

RAAZ AGLE JANAM KA?

Question: What is the spiritual perspective on the recent popular serial *Raaz Pichhle Janam Ka* (The Secret of Previous Life)?

Answer: The serial brought the much-neglected topic of reincarnation to the forefront of the public mind. That, in and of itself, is a significant and positive development. For too long has reincarnation been relegated to the realm of a sectarian, sentimental and religious belief. Reincarnation is not just a Hindu or Buddhist belief; verses confirming it can be found in all the great religions of the world including Christianity, Islam and Judaism, as is persuasively presented in several well-researched books including ISKCON scholar Steven Rosen's landmark book *The Reincarnation Controversy.*

Even in science, bold researchers like Dr Ian Stevenson have accumulated strong evidence supporting reincarnation. That's why both in the east and the west, books on reincarnation are becoming increasingly popular. The serial *Raaz Pichhle Janam Ka* was an example of this phenomenon.

One problem with such popular renditions is that they often romanticize and sensationalize reincarnation, thus distracting people from its serious implications. Many people fancifully imagine about their past life and some even try out past-life regressions. Such regressions may give factually accurate information about the person's past life. They may free people from phobias caused by past-life traumas. But they can do nothing to save us from future traumas – in this life and the next. We still have to undergo the trauma of old age, disease and death in this very life. And as souls who will take another body in our future life, we will have to undergo these traumas again and again. Unless we try to understand *Raaz Agle Janam Ka* (The Secret of the Next Life).

This secret is clearly explained in the *Bhagavad-gita* (8.4-5) in terms of the law of last thought. Whatever is our last thought while dying becomes the template on which our next body is built. So an intelligent person chooses to think, at the time of death, of God and of one's eternal relationship with him. Thus one can gain an eternal spiritual body in God's kingdom, where one goes beyond all bodily traumas. But we can't think of God at the time of death without practice; our last thought will generally be about our deepest attachment - wealth, estate, spouse, children or whatever. Therefore, we need to practice thinking of God during our life by chanting his holy names like the Hare Krishna mantra. Then we can reclaim our lost eternal life, which is the highest benefit of the knowledge of reincarnation.

The serial tries to illuminate the past; the *Gita* illuminates the future. It's for us to pick the *raaz* that matters most to us.

Toward Self-Empowerment

CONQUER FEAR

Question: Can spirituality help one to become free from anxiety and fear?

Answer: Surely.

To understand how, let's begin with a thought exercise.

Suppose you are walking on a lonely street late at night. Suddenly you see a hefty, suspicious-looking person charging toward you. Just as fear starts creeping up your spine, you notice an armed policeman standing on guard nearby. Immediately your fear disappears.

Like in the above story, all of us are on a journey through the street of life. At any moment, problems – financial, familial, social, educational, professional, physical – may charge upon us. These problems – even their very thoughts – trigger fear within us. But if we are able to see the Lord always by our side, ready to protect us whenever required, then our fears will subside. The *Bhagavad-gita* (5.29) describes that the Lord is always present in our hearts, but we need to refine our devotional vision to perceive his presence there. Two quick and effective ways to feel God's protective presence are praying to him and chanting his holy names.

Another way to overcome fear is by illumining ourselves with spiritual wisdom. When we enter a dark room, we imagine various dangers within it and so feel fearful. But when we turn on the light, we see our fears to be baseless. Similarly, when we are spiritually uninformed, life is like a dark room for us and so we often imagine things going wrong in the future and make ourselves fearful. When we turn on the light of divine wisdom in our own hearts, we understand our own spiritual identity as eternal souls who are forever beyond destruction. This understanding of our core indestructibility enables us to dismiss most of our fears as the baseless imaginations of our paranoid minds.

Ultimately, courage comes not by the mere absence of fear, but by absorption in a cause that takes us beyond fear. When we are inspired by a great cause, a cause far greater than ourselves, our fears about protecting our own petty concerns evaporate. The greatest of all causes is the selfless devotional service of the Lord. Why? Because the Lord is the greatest well wisher of all living beings, and so, by serving his will, we can do the greatest good to one and all – including, of course, our own selves. A shining example of fearlessness through absorption in sharing God's love with the world is Srila Prabhupada. At the age of 69, when most people fear going across a street alone, Srila Prabhupada went across the oceans to America, alone and penniless. Within eleven short years, he built 108 temples, wrote over 70 books, and circumnavigated the globe 14 times on lecture-tours and inspired millions of people toward a wisdom-based life of fearlessness.

IS SPIRITUALITY PRACTICAL?

Question: In our fast-paced modern life, is spirituality practical?

Answer: Certainly.

No matter how fast-paced our life becomes, the practical purpose of all our activities always remains happiness. Spirituality reveals to us the best form of happiness, a happiness that can never be taken away from us. The Vedic texts explain that as souls, we all have an eternal loving relationship with the all-attractive Supreme Lord. In loving and serving God, we can relish supreme and everlasting happiness; the more we love God, the happier we become.

Love for God is sometimes thought of as impractical because it directs our vision to the other world, the eternal spiritual world beyond the temporary material world. But this other-worldly goal does not make us impractical; rather, it builds the most solid foundation for living practically in this world. Just as when we switch on the master switch in a house, all the lights in the house automatically turn on, similarly, when we awaken our love for God, our love for all living beings automatically awakens. We realize that all of us are brothers and sisters in the one universal family of God. When we love all living beings, we no longer desire to exploit or manipulate them for our selfish interests. Instead, our love for God inspires us to love and serve each other. This creates a culture of

 warmth, trust and service, which makes practical life joyful. This contrasts sharply with the modern culture of alienation, suspicion and exploitation, which makes practical life joyless.

When we follow a genuine spiritual path,

even in its early stages, it activates our latent spiritual perception. We intuitively realize that God is our greatest well-wisher and is in charge of our lives. So we understand that whatever happens in our life is sanctioned by him and is for our ultimate good, even if it seems all wrong to us. Without this realization of God's benevolent orchestration of our life, the seemingly chaotic events of life often become impractical and impossible to manage. But equipped with divine vision, we no longer feel life to be an impractical, losing battle against a hostile world. Rather, we recognize difficulties as concealed opportunities for practical growth.

We may still fear, "All these benefits sound great, but is following a spiritual path to get these benefits practical?" Why not? All we have to do is associate with saintly people, study books of wisdom like the *Bhagavad-gita* and chant the holy names of God like the Hare Krishna mahamantra. Thus the path is practical and easy, and the results too are practical and beneficial. So let's rid ourselves of this misconception that spirituality is impractical.

THE POWER OF DIVINE SOUND

Question: In the Vedic tradition, there seems to be a lot of emphasis on spiritual sound vibrations, on hearing from a spiritual master. Why this emphasis?

Answer: Sonic technology is central to the Vedic program of spiritual redemption. That's why the Vedanta-sutra, the condensed conclusion of all Vedic wisdom, culminates in the aphorism: *anavrittih shabdat* "The uncovering of pure consciousness occurs by divine sound."

 The Vedic texts explain that all of us are afflicted by spiritual amnesia. As spiritual beings, we are eternal and indestructible. But due to forgetting our spiritual identity, we live in anxiety and fear caused by the fragility and mortality of our material bodies. As parts of God, we are intrinsically joyful like him, but due to having forgotten our internal connection with him, we struggle for paltry pleasures in the external world. Overall, our spiritual forgetfulness causes us to be shackled by trivial desires and fears, thus making us live far below our potentials.

The guru is like an expert doctor who can cure our spiritual amnesia. When the guru is himself a devotee dedicated to the service of the Lord and when he repeats the message of God as given in the scriptures, then his words of wisdom have a special spiritual potency. Those words, called as *shabda brahma* (God manifested as sound vibration), penetrate all the material coverings on the soul, thus reviving one's spiritual memory. Thus the words of the guru stand in marked contrast to all other ordinary words, which simply get incorporated into and increase the layers of forgetfulness that cover the soul.

As we have been living in spiritual forgetfulness for many, many lifetimes, reviving our spiritual memory may take some time, just as curing a chronic disease may take some time. But the result we get on being cured – becoming free from the limitations of our bodies and minds and rejoicing in the life of freedom and love that is our original nature – is well-worth the effort and the patience

The unleashing power of divine sound is illustrated in the *Ramayana*, which, in addition to describing real events that took place in remote history, also demonstrates timeless, universal truths. In the *Ramayana*, the simian-hero, *Hanuman*, plays a relatively minor role till being spiritually aroused by the words of wisdom of the veteran-warrior, Jambavan, who acts like a spiritual mentor. Thereafter Hanuman's profile changes dramatically, and he does astounding feats in the service of Rama. Similarly, whatever be our achievements – minor or major – before we hear the words of wisdom from a guru, all those achievements will pale into insignificance as we rise to new levels of fulfillment and accomplishment in our real life of devotional service to the Lord and all his children.

ॐ

WHY IRRATIONAL SHOPPING?

Question: When shopping, why do many intelligent people suddenly become almost irrational and purchase dozens of unnecessary and even unwanted things?

Answer: The *Bhagavad-gita* (2.62-63) describes the psychological cause of such irrational behavior:

"Dwelling on sense objects causes lust to catch on fire.

Lust produces anger, born of unfulfilled desire.

Anger breeds confusion and bewilders memory,

Causing lost intelligence and endless misery."

Let's understand this verse through the analogy of a snowball.

Through catchy sponsorship tags, jazzy billboards and dazzling TV commercials, the advertising industry brings consumer products in front of our senses again and again. And almost all advertisements try to catch our attention by depicting the female form at various imagination-triggering levels of dressing or undressing.

John enters a supermarket and his senses are immediately bombarded by sights, smells and sounds of lifestyle products, products that are not on his shopping list. Contemplation on those stimuli creates in his mind a small pebble of desire, lust. As the pebble keeps rolling down in his mind, the initial "That's nice" feeling soon becomes an irresistible "I want it" craving. Then a sudden wave of fury "Who can stop me from getting it?" sweeps across his mind. The resulting confusion sabotages his memory of his recent resolution to not spend needlessly. With the memory knocked down, the emotional snowball then crushes the intelligence, thus wrecking the last defense against irrationality.

Purchasing an extra product might not appear such a serious problem, but what if it becomes an addiction?

And the emotional snowball principle can be exploited for far greater kinds of irrationality. By seducing gullible young men with promises of virgins in paradise, vested interests convert them into suicide bombers.

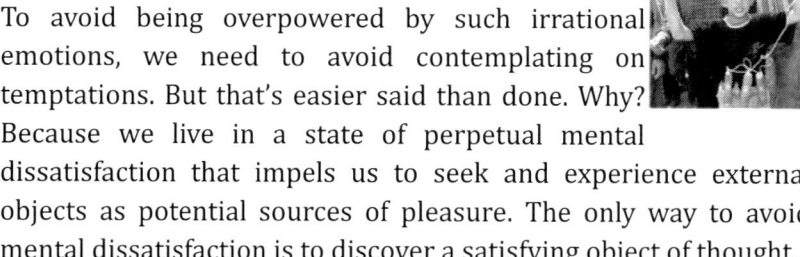

To avoid being overpowered by such irrational emotions, we need to avoid contemplating on temptations. But that's easier said than done. Why? Because we live in a state of perpetual mental dissatisfaction that impels us to seek and experience external objects as potential sources of pleasure. The only way to avoid mental dissatisfaction is to discover a satisfying object of thought.

The Vedic tradition reveals God to be Krishna, the supremely beautiful, supremely powerful, supremely wealthy, supremely wise, supremely peaceful, supremely famous person. Due to his all-attractive, all-loving nature, Krishna is the most satisfying object of thought. And the easiest and best way to think about Krishna is by chanting his holy names like the Hare Krishna mahamantra. By cultivating the practice of regular chanting, we can make thoughts about Krishna our default thoughts and thus experience constant internal satisfaction. Then, whether we are shopping or doing any other activity, instead of being crushed by the emotional snowball, we can crush it in its formative stage – while it is still a pebble.

෪

How do Saints Help Others?

Question: The Indian culture, like most traditional cultures, recommends associating with saints. How does such association practically help us?

Answer: The German poet Goethe said, "Treat a man as he is and he will remain as he is. Treat a man as he can and should be and he will

become as he can and should be." Most of us have a tendency to focus on people's faults and stick labels like "lazy", "short-tempered" and "immoral" on them. When we harp on people's faults, we force them into a defensive, justifying mode. This distracts them from doing the deep internal work that can bring out their divine potential.

In marked contrast, saints help bring out the good in others, for they know everyone to be potentially divine. Let's see two saints in action.

Once, the great saint Ramanujacharya (ca. 1017 to 1137), while in the sacred town of Srirangam, came across a young man, Dhanur das, who was completely infatuated by a society girl and was fanning her in public. In those days, such behavior was scandalous, and people were condemning him for his shamelessness, but he was oblivious to their criticisms. Seeing him as a pure soul temporarily covered by illusion, Ramanujacharya politely asked him why he was so attracted to that woman. Dhanur das replied passionately, "I have never seen eyes as beautiful as hers." Appreciating his earnest love for beauty, Ramanujacharya challenged him, "What would you do if I showed you eyes far more beautiful than these?" Dhanur das promptly replied, "I would devote myself to the person with those eyes." Ramanujacharya took him to the magnificent temple of Lord Ranganath and showed him the beautiful deity form there. By Ramanujacharya's sincerer prayers, the Lord revealed the supreme beauty of his eyes to Dhanur das. Mesmerized by that divine beauty, Dhanur das fell in love with the Lord and went on to become a saintly devotee.

Srila Prabhupada went to America during the 1960s, the period of the counterculture. At that time, thousands of youths were becoming "hippies", seeking "to go high", to have spiritual  experiences, by taking drugs. Srila Prabhupada did not decry them for being useless addicts as the American mainstream was doing, but he compassionately fanned the spark of spiritual interest that they had. He lovingly explained to them how mantra chanting – and not drugs – would enable them to "stay high forever", to rise to a high, fulfilling, lasting state of constant spiritual experiences. Encouraged and guided by him, many of his students have become internationally respected spiritual leaders, selflessly sharing God's love with one and all.

Thus, saints help bring out our latent divine qualities and so their association should be cherished as a precious blessing and a glorious opportunity.

སོ

LUST & LOVE: WHAT'S THE DIFFERENCE?

Question: What is the difference between lust and love?

Answer: The difference is huge, but is hardly understood. Mistaking lust to be love can be said to be the essential tragedy of modern society. Lust sees the other person as an object for one's own enjoyment, whereas love sees the other person as a person to be served and pleased. The sixteenth century devotional classic Chaitanya Charitamrita compares love to gold and lust to copper. If copper is gold-coated, the uninformed mistake it to be gold. Similarly, if lust is covered with smiles, flatteries and gifts, the undiscriminating mistake it to be love.

Lust originates from the fundamental ignorance of our own identity. When we mistake ourselves to be physical bodies, whether male or female, we naturally come under the control of bodily drives for lusty pleasures. Lust creates within us a hunger for matter, which we struggle to fulfill by exploiting another person's body for our pleasure. But lusty pleasures are treacherously anticlimactic; fantasies cherished for years fizzle out in minutes. So, when relationships are formed based on lust, as happens often in so-called "love" marriages, those relationships are soon wrecked by the selfishness inherent in lust.

True love begins with a clear understanding of our spiritual identity. The *Bhagavad-gita* describes that we are spiritual beings, beloved parts of the Supreme All-Attractive Being, Krishna. In our pure state, we innately love Krishna and delight eternally in that eternal love. When Krishna – the source and pivot of all love – is at the center of our heart and life, then we naturally love all living beings, for we see them as beloved children of our Lord. When our relationships are thus divinely-centered, then we can relish and share true love.

But when we turn away from Krishna, we forget our spiritual identity and misidentify with our temporary bodily coverings. That misidentification perverts our natural love for Krishna into an unnatural lust for matter. Often, this perversion sabotages our intelligence so thoroughly that we start mistaking carnal lust to be natural and spiritual love to be unnatural. Only when we come in touch with saints who have transformed their lust into love can we recognize and remedy our unnatural predicament. Lust being a perversion of our original, essential nature, can be reverted to love for Krishna through the scientific process of mantra meditation. Krishna being omnipotent is fully present in his Holy Names like the Hare Krishna mahamantra. Meditatively chanting the Holy Names therefore connects us immediately with Krishna, who is love personified and so awakens our divine love. By saintly association and mantra meditation, we can transform lust into love and thus reclaim our original life of endless love.

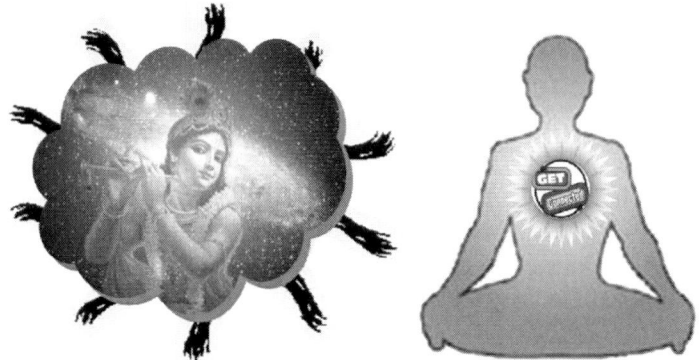

౸

BEAT THE THIEF, NOT THE WATCHDOG

Question: Why do some people commit horrible crimes without the slightest remorse? Do they have no conscience?

Answer: Our conscience is like our internal watchdog. It barks and warns us whenever the thief of immorality comes to plunder our integrity. Those who heed the

watchdog's warning drive away the thief; they reject the immoral temptation by activating their intelligence. Others get so allured by the temptation that they beat the dog instead of the thief! They silence the voice of their conscience and delight in immoral pleasures.

The *Bhagavad-gita* (15.15) explains that the Lord personally resides in our hearts as the Supersoul (Paramatma) to guide us in our life's journey. Our conscience, when pure, is actually the voice of God guiding from within. When a person knowingly and repeatedly acts contrary to the inner voice, he is telling God by his actions: "I will to do what I want to; I don't want your guidance." Due to this adamance and defiance, God withdraws his guidance; the inner voice starts fading till it becomes almost mute. Then that person unhesitatingly does unconscionable acts.

Some examples of people with muted conscience are animal slaughterers, criminal sociopaths, rapists, child abusers and mercenary murderers. Terrorists have not only muted the voice of the true God who loves all his children, but have also imagined a god who hates those whom they hate. Thus, the "god" of the terrorists is a fabrication of their own ego, created to provide a religious rationalization for their irrational malevolence.

We are all free to neglect the inner voice, but we cannot neglect the consequences of that neglect. If a person driving a car on a steep mountainous road breaks the fencing at the side of the road and thinks, "Now I can freely enjoy riding the way I want," his freedom will simply become a free-fall to destruction. Similar is the plight of those who break the  fences that God has created on the road that takes us back to Him. For example, those who break God-given regulations for sexual morality freely fall to various sufferings, with sexually transmitted diseases (STDs) like AIDS, syphilis, gonorrhea being the most obvious among them.

For those of us whose conscience may be somewhat muted, can we raise its volume again? Certainly. God guides us not only internally as the Supersoul, but also externally through *guru-sadhu-shastra* (spiritual master - saintly teachers - sacred scriptures). When we follow their external guidance, we show God that we do want his internal guidance. He naturally reciprocates by making the voice of conscience louder. Empowered by that inner guidance, we can all gradually become exemplary human beings having the highest moral and spiritual integrity.

ॐ

"I AM NOT AFRAID OF DEATH"

Question: I have seen that spiritualists often have a standard message: material life is temporary with death possible at any time, so we should enquire about eternal life without delay. Why do they use death as a tool to scare people into taking up religious practice? Anyway, nobody can do that to me because I am not afraid of death.

Answer: I appreciate your concern and would like to present a few thoughts for your consideration.

If you hear a spouse telling his / her partner: 'I don't care about our relationship ending', what does this statement suggest? It could suggest that the spouse is not happy with the relationship, doesn't value it much and so doesn't care about ending it. Or if someone says, 'I don't care if my car is burnt in riots,' it could mean he doesn't value the car. Similarly, if somebody says, 'I am not afraid of losing my life,' it could mean that he is not enjoying life, doesn't value it much and so doesn't care about losing it. So the bravado about being unafraid of death could indicate frustration with life.

Moreover, this bravado of being unafraid of death generally lasts only till one is face-to-face with imminent death. Then one fearfully and desperately tries everything possible to avoid death. But, by then, it's too late.

Spiritualists feel sad to see people needlessly cut such a sorry figure at the time of death. So they tirelessly strive to share the universal truths of life that can empower one to value life and value death. What are those truths? We are all eternal, indestructible souls, beloved children of God, Krishna, and are entitled to live forever with Him in everlasting bliss. But because we are mistaking ourselves to be our mortal bodies, we are subjecting ourselves to the sufferings of death – life after life.

Spiritualists live in harmony with God by chanting His holy names and offering their love to Him and so they experience peace and joy even in this life. Consequently, they truly value life: not the illusory life wasted in pursuing temporary pleasures, but the real life led in loving harmony with God. And they value death too; death reminds them of the urgency of reclaiming their eternal lives.

Hare Kṛṣṇa, Hare Kṛṣṇa
Kṛṣṇa Kṛṣṇa, Hare Hare
Hare Rāma, Hare Rāma
Rāma Rāma, Hare Hare

Most people are so captivated by hopes of temporary pleasures that they neglect their right to eternal life. So, just as a doctor is duty-bound to alert a cancer-afflicted patient about the disease's future course, a spiritualist feels duty-bound to alert mortality-afflicted people about their imminent deaths. This is not a scaring technique, but an alerting technique. Fear of death doesn't spoil the joy of life; rather it points the way to the real joy of life.

ॐ

Take IT to the Next Level

Question: India has proven its mettle by its remarkable contributions in IT (Information Technology). Why does India need spirituality in this IT age?

Answer: The IT boom over the last decade has made India a global power to reckon with. But the recent global recession has raised a hard question: In spite of our knowledge of global markets and how to manipulate them, why did we have to reel under a global market crash that our IT systems could not predict and had to struggle to cope with? It's because IT has some fundamental limitations that are often overlooked:

Information is not insight: Information dazzles us with facts and figures, while distracting us from deeper truths that illuminate and enrich, truths about our origin, identity, value and purpose.

Technology debilitates our spirit: Technology makes us so fascinated and dependent on external gadgetry that we forget to develop ourselves, to realize our mental and spiritual potentials.

These limitations of IT have become even more critical in our times when IT is being used by the consumerist society to aggravate people's greed for materialistic pleasures and possessions. For example, human greed caused the US sub-prime crisis, but the global IT networks expanded that crisis into a worldwide economic meltdown. Sadly but predictably, IT has ended up consolidating an exploitative, selfish world order, which inflicts poverty and scarcity on millions, rapes mother nature and robs future generations of their rightful natural resources.

To wisely use IT, we need another IT: Inner Transformation. What

INNER TRANSFORMATION

the world needs especially today is not improved information technology, but effective inner transformation technology that will enable people to use IT constructively. India has a rich, unparalleled tradition of time-honored spiritual practices like mantra meditation that can bring about inner transformation, thus empowering people to experience spiritual happiness and freeing them from greed.

Noble Laureate Chemist Dr Richard Ernst points this out, "I am convinced that India could become once again the cradle of a new school of thought that may significantly influence the fate of the globe in the third millennium. Perhaps the contributions of India to nuclear power technology and space science will turn out to be irrelevant, but the contributions  towards a new ethical foundation could be turning the wheel of history in the proper (balanced) way."

In the same spirit, more than three decades before Ernst's observation, Srila Prabhupada, the founder of ISKCON, went to USA, and boldly announced that he had come there not to beg for money or technology like many Indian political leaders had in the past; he had come instead to share spiritual wisdom. Due to his confidence in the relevance of of India's spiritual legacy, millions of peeople have learnt - and are learning - the ultimate IT and are pioneering a more balanced world. If more Indians could imbibe this spirit, and assimilate and disseminate her national spiritual legacy, India could lead the world in taking IT to the next level.

HEAD + HEART = HAPPINESS?

Question: Intellectual people tend to be unfeeling, whereas emotional people tend to be irrational. Can a person be both intellectual and emotional simultaneously?

Answer: A satisfying, effective life requires the harmony of both thought and emotion. When thought dominates emotion, one becomes unfeeling, hard-hearted, and life becomes listless and boring. When emotion dominates thought, one becomes moody – violent or depressed – and life goes out of control.

Ideally, thought should be enlivened by emotion and emotion should be directed and regulated by thought. This blend is taught by Lord Krishna in the *Bhagavad-gita*. At the start of the *Gita*, Arjuna's emotions overpowered his thoughts, thus making him falter in his warrior dharma of protecting the citizens from atrocious rulers. Krishna's words of wisdom, which taught the difference between the temporary body and the eternal soul, stimulated Arjuna's rational faculty, thus helping him gain control over his emotions. But Krishna's guidance didn't stop there. His teaching of bhakti-yoga – the eternal loving relationship between the soul and God – ushered Arjuna into the world of divine emotions. There, Arjuna learnt, all activity is done not just as a duty, but as an expression of one's devotion to help enact God's will in this world for the good of all. That's why Krishna repeatedly exhorts Arjuna to serve with both his mind and his intelligence, that is, both his emotion and his thought.

Today, our educational system teaches us practically nothing about the philosophical aspect of life. Consequently, most people know no ultimate purpose of life; their thoughts remain caught in satisfying stray emotional urges created by advertisements and media. Thus they lead hurried yet dissatisfied lives, driven by irrational impulses and unquenchable desires. When these emotions go out of control, they transmogrify into irrational violence against others as in vandalism and murder, or irrational violence against themselves as in suicide.

With the neglect of the religious aspect, the inbuilt self-restraint that religious morality teaches has also been done away with. No wonder we see so many people being hijacked by their emotions.

Just as Arjuna turned to Krishna to save himself from irrational emotions, so can we. Even if we feel that our emotions are not out of control at present, by learning from Krishna, we can equip ourselves to face the inevitable future emotional turbulences. All of us need to not only bring rational thought in control of irrational emotion, but also to let divine emotion enliven rational thought. Divine emotion is easily invoked by chanting the holy names of God like the Hare Krishna maha-mantra, for chanting reawakens our divine love for God.

With the anchors of philosophy and meditation, all of us can sail safely through the stormy ocean of irrational emotions to the shores of eternal devotion.

೮౩

DOES SPIRITUALITY KILL AMBITION?

Question: Bhakti, with its emphasis on prayer, submission and surrender to God, seems very anti-ambitious and anti-heroic. Doesn't this make a devotee weak and unambitious?

Answer: Not at all.

All of us have a desire to do something special, wonderful, heroic. But most people fail to go beyond daydreaming. The few who are talented and dedicated and fortunate enough succeed in becoming heroes – but only for a distressingly brief period. As age catches up with them, their degenerating bodies and declining talents let them down and their heroism slips away inexorably. Finally death makes heroes into zeroes – as souls with nothing at all, who then have to go to their next bodies where they restart their permanently doomed quest for heroism.

Bhakti-yoga offers us a positive alternative in our quest for heroism. If we try to do something heroic in service of the supreme hero, God, then that heroism does lasting good to ourselves and to others. For example, if we have musical talent and compose devotional music that brings our own hearts and others' hearts closer to God, then that increased proximity to God will give us far deeper fulfillment than fame as a popular musician. Additionally, through our music, we will share with others not just fleeting mundane entertainment but lasting spiritual fulfillment. Moreover, if we sincerely glorify God with our existing talent, he may increase that talent manifold so that we can do more good for the world. Last and far from the least, even if we have only modest talent, still glorifying God with that talent will give us far greater satisfaction than what the most talented musician will get by composing popular worldly music.

By glorifying God with whatever talents and resources we have, all of us can become heroes. We may or may not make headlines in the public eyes, but we will make headlines in God's eyes and will do real good to others, which is the essence of true heroism. Lord Krishna calls upon Arjuna to become a spiritual hero in the *Bhagavad-gita* (11.33), "Therefore get up. Prepare to fight and win glory. Conquer your enemies and enjoy a flourishing kingdom. They are already put to death by my arrangement, so be an instrument in the fight."

Consider the example of the quintessential *bhakta*: Hanuman. He is assertive, intelligent, resourceful, dynamic and powerful. Hanuman is no doubt a servant of the supreme hero Rama, but he is also a hero in his own right. Hanuman is often depicted with folded palms holding a mace. The folded palms symbolize *bhakti* (devotion), and the mace symbolizes *shakti* (power). Thus, by  personifying the paradoxical blend of *bhakti* and *shakti*, Hanuman invites each one of us to devotionally fulfill our dream of heroism.

ॐ

Vedic Insights

CAN GOD MAKE A SQUARE CIRCLE?

Question: If God can do anything, can he make a square circle?

Answer: Questions like these arise from not understanding the implications of God's omnipotency. To understand how nothing is impossible for God, let's consider the two kinds of impossibilities: practical and logical.

Practical impossibility: When the sacred scriptures describe that, say, Lord Krishna lifted the huge Govardhana hill in Vrindavana during his descent to this world five thousand years ago, skeptics may dismiss this as a fantasy, because they deem possession of such strength to be practically impossible. However, notice their self-centric mentality implicitly operating here; they presume that what 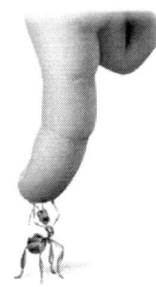 is impossible for them is impossible for everyone. By such a mentality, an ant crawling on a table may consider the glass that blocks its way impossible to lift, but we humans do it all the time – nonchalantly. Just as we, humans, being much stronger than ants, can do what they think to be practically impossible, similarly, God, being infinitely stronger than us, can do what we think to be practically impossible.

Logical impossibility: Activities like making a square circle seem not just practically impossible, but even logically impossible. Our mind tends to think that a geometrical object can either be a circle or a square, but never both. However, this is a limitation of our mind, not a limitation of God. Our mind functions by discerning in the world around us features like logicality, causality and repeatability. It needs the intellectual framework formed by such attributes to make sense of the world. But that very framework limits it from "thinking outside the box", so we mistakenly infer that activities which are impossible for us to think logically must also be impossible for God to do practically. However, our framework of thought limits us, not God. For his cognition, God does not need any such framework; therefore, he is completely free to think and act independent of it.

Let's now apply this background analysis to our specific question: can God make a square circle? Certainly, he can. But our minds can never understand how. Is this an evasive answer? Not at all. The sixteenth-century devotee-scholar Jiva Goswami insightfully reminds us that if God's actions were limited to the conceiving abilities of our mind, then our mind would be supreme, not God, thus violating the very definition of God. Therefore, by his very definition, God has inconceivability (achintyatva in Sanskrit) as his integral attribute. Based on this principle of inconceivability, Srila Prabhupada brilliantly answered a standard skeptical question:

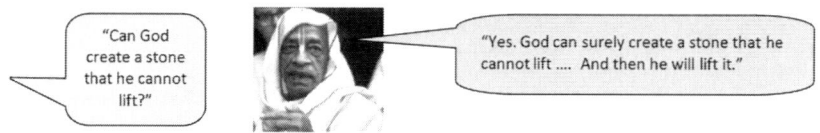

ॐ

WHY DOES GOD DEMAND FAITH?

Question: If God exists, why does he not reveal himself to us? Why does he first demand faith before we can know and see him?

Answer: When we ask a question like this, we often forget that acquiring even worldly knowledge requires faith and training. Let's consider a few examples:

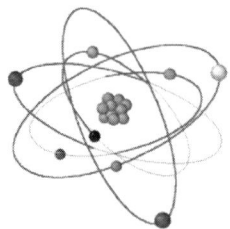

1.   If we were to ask a group of people, "Do you believe in the existence of a lepton or a baryon?" most people would give us an uncomprehending look. Those who know that these terms refer to subatomic particles will say, "Scientists say – and so I believe – that these particles exist." Such deference to scientific authority for matters beyond ordinary jurisdiction is reasonable and desirable.

Yet to the question, "Do you believe in the existence of God?" almost all people in the same group will express some opinion; the atheists will be assertive, even aggressive, despite the fact that this question is far beyond their jurisdiction. Worse, they will condemn deference to spiritual authority as blind faith.

2. Consider the incomprehensibility of the cutting edge branch of quantum physics. Noble Laureate physicist Richard Feynman states, "[our current physics] describes nature as absurd from the point of view of common sense. And it agrees fully with experiment. So I hope you can accept nature as she is – absurd." A quantum physics student has to accept on faith that the universe is filled with particles that are intrinsically unobservable and undergo training for eight to ten years before he can begin

comprehending quantum reality. Yet when spiritual teachers ask for something similar: accept the existence of God and train yourself through material regulation and spiritual meditation to experience higher reality, objections abound, "Why  should I follow any rules? All this is unscientific." An atheist giving an argument like this is similar to a judge declaring the verdict before even starting the hearing of the case.

Such blatant double standards beg the question: Is no training, no qualification needed to pass judgment on spiritual matters? ISKCON founder-acharya Srila Prabhupada, during his talk at MIT (Massachusetts Institute of Technology), famously asked, "In MIT, why is there no department to study the almighty?"

It required years, decades and centuries of sustained training and effort for us to begin comprehending God's creation through science. God is the profoundest and loftiest of all things and beings and is far greater than his creation. Then why should we object to the little training and effort that is necessary to comprehend God through spirituality?

When we understand God's exalted position, we will recognize that his demand for faith is not at all unreasonable; rather it is our demand to see him without reposing any faith or taking any training that is unreasonable.

౮

LOVE WINS OVER LOGIC

Question: If God is omniscient, then he knows how he is going to act to change the future course of history using his omnipotence. But that implies he can't change his mind about his future actions, which means he is not omnipotent. So doesn't this mean that God can either be omnipotent or omniscient, but not both?

Answer: Questions like these arise when we approach God only with our head and not our heart. We then mistake God to be a static, unconscious object and his attributes to be like the length, breadth, height, mass etc of that object. But God is not an object; he is a conscious, loving person. Over and above his omnipotence and omniscience, God has an even more fundamental defining attribute: omni-benevolence. Omni-benevolence means that God is the supreme well-wisher and benefactor of all living beings, as is proclaimed in the *Bhagavad-gita* (5.29). God does not delight in

 displaying his omnipotence or omniscience; he delights in reciprocating love with those who love him and in extending his love to those who don't love him. So according to how he can best benefit all living beings, he sometimes exhibits his omnipotence, sometimes his omniscience, sometimes both and sometimes neither. Consider the *Mahabharata* incident when Lord Krishna went as a peace messenger to the evil-minded Duryodhana to avoid the fratricidal war. Seen superficially, Krishna failed in his mission: he couldn't persuade Duryodhana. Was Krishna not omnipotent? He was, but he did not exercise his omnipotence because he respected the free will of Duryodhana. Was Krishna not omniscient

to know in advance that Duryodhana would not accept his peace proposal? He was, but he did not exercise his omniscience. Why? Firstly, he wanted to express his love for the Pandavas by accepting the undistinguished role of a messenger for their sake. Secondly, he wanted to do all he could to avoid the war and thus show his loving concern for all – not only the innocent masses who would suffer the effects of the war, but also the malevolent miscreants who had incited it. On other occasions in the same Mahabharata, Krishna exhibited his omniscience in protecting the Pandavas from the empowered arrows of Bhishma, his omnipotence in foiling Duryodhana's attempt to arrest him by displaying his universal form, and both his omnipotence and omniscience in helping Arjuna to avenge the unjust murder of his son. Love is what motivates the  Lord to perform these often-puzzling activities, and love is what will enable us to figure out the puzzles. So let's remember, if we want to understand the Lord, we need to subordinate our logic to our love.

೮೦

SPIRITUAL HAPPINESS: A MYSTERY?

Question: Although the scriptures and saints glorify spiritual happiness as oceanic, many people are unable to experience even a drop of that happiness. Why?

Answer: Because of misdirected vision.

Here's an example to understand the blinding effect of misdirected vision. Suppose a person stares at the back side of a canvas. Will he be able to appreciate the beauty of the painting? No, even if he scrutinizes it for hours or even years. Nor will he understand why connoisseurs of art are delighting over it; indeed, he may even call them crazy. Suppose the art connoisseurs are in minority; how will they communicate the beauty of the painting to the unsympathetic majority?

Like the art connoisseurs in this hypothetical example, the spiritual connoisseurs – the devotees who delight in remembering their beloved Lord, Sri Krishna – are considered strange, even crazy, by others. The joy they derive in singing the praises of the Lord – often in public kirtans – is incomprehensible not only for many onlookers but also for scholars with doctorates in religion.

This mystery of this simultaneous accessibility and inaccessibility of spiritual happiness is unraveled in the *Bhagavad-gita* (15.11): "The transcendentalists who strive to situate themselves on the spiritual platform can see the soul clearly. But others who are not spiritually situated cannot see the soul even if they try, because their consciousness is misdirected." For those pursuing worldly pleasures and possessions, their infatuation with matter blinds them to spiritual reality. Even if they study spiritual literature, they are unable to even touch spiritual happiness because their minds are filled with dreams and schemes for materialistic enjoyment. Their endeavors to understand spirituality are in vain, like the attempts of a blind man to see by squinting and straining his eyes.

But the blind man is not condemned to permanent blindness; he can see if he agrees to follow the doctor. Similarly, materialists are not condemned to perpetual spiritual deprivation; they can experience spiritual bliss if they agree to follow the supreme doctor, Lord Krishna. Krishna's therapy for redirecting their consciousness from matter to spirit involves:

1. Avoiding materially entangling activities:

Four activities that especially entangle our minds in matter are gambling, intoxication, meat-eating and illicit sex. By shunning these activities, we will find our consciousness becoming clearer and sharper to perceive spiritual truths.

2. Maximizing spiritually absorbing activities:

Learning spiritual principles and values by associating with devotees, studying scriptures like the Bhagavad-gita and chanting the holy name of God connects us practically and joyfully with God, the reservoir of all spiritual bliss.

By patiently and diligently following this twofold process, all of us can, figuratively speaking, turn our vision from the back of the canvas to the front, and thus experience spiritual bliss.

ॐ

HANDWRITING ANALYSIS
OF A DOCTOR'S PRESCRIPTION

Question: If one wants to understand scriptures systematically, how helpful are academic degrees in religious studies?

Answer: Not much.

 Imagine that a calligraphy expert takes a doctor's prescription from a patient and starts doing its handwriting analysis. Then he starts broadcasting his analysis: "The way 'j' is written indicates a South Indian style, the way 'w' is curved indicates a Bengali background…" Distracted by the calligrapher, the patient forgets to follow the prescription and stays sick.

Sounds absurd? Sometimes the academic study of scriptures can be just as absurd. Let's see how.

We are all souls, beloved children of God, who are suffering from spiritual amnesia. We have forgotten our spiritual identity and are mistaking ourselves to be material bodies. By our very nature, we constantly thirst for pleasure. Due to our amnesia, we misdirect this thirst to temporary material objects and so miss out on the eternal spiritual happiness that is our birthright.

To help us reclaim our birthright, the supreme physician, God, Krishna, gives his prescription in scriptures like the Bhagavad-gita. The Gita prescribes the scientific process of bhakti-yoga to revive our spiritual memory by sustained and systematic devotional stimuli. Millions of people throughout history and thousands even today have healed themselves through the *Gita's* prescription.

What's the proof that they are healed, that they have found spiritual happiness? The proof is that they have become free from addiction to self-defeating pleasures like illicit sex and intoxication, pleasures which captivate those with no access to spiritual happiness. Thus the Gita's prescription works.

But most academic scholars neglect the *Gita's* prescription and focus instead on its textual analysis. For example, they may analyze the Sanskrit style of different verses and ascribe different ages to them. In fact, they do everything with the *Gita* except what the *Gita* is telling them repeatedly to do: cultivate  devotional remembrance of Krishna. No wonder they miss the whole purpose of the *Gita*. That's why Lord Krishna forewarns: "The envious, who don't follow my teachings, are baffled, despite all their knowledge. Know that their consciousness is misdirected." (*Gita* 4.32) Of course, Lord Krishna does not condemn scholarship itself; elsewhere in the Gita (18.70), he proclaims study of the *Gita* to be divine worship. What he condemns is lopsided scholarship that only analyzes the knowledge, but never applies the knowledge.

The contrasting effects of the academic and devotional approaches to Gita study are dramatically demonstrated through modern history. Till 1970, several hundred academic scholars wrote Gita commentaries, but hardly anyone – neither author nor reader – adopted devotional practices. But since 1970, when Srila Prabhupada, a pre-eminent devotee-scholar, published his *Bhagavad-gita As It Is*, over four million people worldwide took up devotional practices and started curing their spiritual amnesia, thus reaping the ultimate benefit of Gita study.

FROM KNOWLEDGE TO REALIZATION

Question: How can we gain practical realization of the knowledge we learn from scriptures?

Answer: Let's first understand how realization is different from knowledge. By spiritual knowledge, we acquire information about the nature of reality; by realization, we acquire experience  about how that information is real. Thus, knowledge is theoretical and intellectual, whereas realization is practical and experiential. Once we have acquired spiritual knowledge, the *Bhagavad-gita* (5.17) describes what we should do next: "By investing one's intelligence, mind, faith and goal in the Supreme, one becomes cleansed of all impurities by spiritual knowledge and proceeds straight on the path of liberation." A clean heart and a one-pointed pursuit of liberation are two symptoms of a person with realization. So realization is the return we get for investing our four human faculties – intelligence, mind, faith and goal – in God. Let's discuss how we can invest these four faculties in God:

1. **Intelligence:** A fanatic may be very showy about his beliefs, but he is exposed when he can't explain those beliefs rationally. He hides his irrationality by aggression – verbal and physical – against those who challenge his beliefs. Such pseudo-spiritual practice without investment of one's intelligence cannot lead to any tangible spiritual realization. Krishna urges Arjuna in the Bhagavad-gita (18.63) to deliberate deeply on the message

spoken and then intelligently choose his course of action. Intelligent spiritual practice is foundational for realization.

2. **Mind:** A ritualistic worshiper may use his intelligence to expertly recite memorized verses, but his mind may well be fixed on the adoration that he hopes to get for his religious performance. Only when his mind is fixed on the Lord whom he is praising with the verses will his recitation lead to realization.

3. **Faith:** A salesman may use both his intelligence and mind to sell a product and earn his living, but he may have no faith that the product will deliver its promised results. But when a devotee exhorts others to chant the names of God, he has complete faith that the holy name will immeasurably benefit the chanters, as is promised in the scriptures.

4. **Goal:** A software engineer may fix his intelligence and mind on his software programs and he may also have faith that the software programs will work, but his goal is not the software program, but the money earned through the programming. A devotee's goal is not any material gain that he expects from God; his goal is  God Himself. He wants to love and serve God eternally.

When we invest all these four core faculties in God, our knowledge blossoms into realization. Then, with a purified heart, we can march steadily and swiftly on the path of liberation and ultimately return to the kingdom of God for a life of everlasting joy.

ॐ

IS GOD MADE IN THE IMAGE OF MAN?

Question: In most temples, we see God depicted in a human form. Isn't this a result of anthropomorphic imagination: because we are humans, we imagine God to have a human form?

Answer: No.

If we think deeply, this idea itself arises due to our self-centered thinking, due to our placing ourselves at the center of things. We think that because we have a humanlike form, we have conceived of God as humanlike. But couldn't the reverse be true? What if God originally had a form and our present human form was modeled according to that original form of God?

The scriptures of the great religions of the world repeatedly refer to God in a personal, humanlike way. For example, the Bible talks about "under His feet" (*Exodus* 24:10); "inscribed with the finger of God" (*Exodus* 31:18); "the hand of the Lord" (*Exodus* 9:3); "the eyes of the Lord" (*Genesis* 38:7); "the ears of the Lord" (*Numbers* 11:1). *Ezekiel* (1:26) describes God as having "the semblance of a human form." Such phrases permeate the biblical literature.

Similarly, in the *Quran*, there are references to "the face of your Lord" (055:027), "under My eye" (020:039), "under our eyes" (052:048) & (054:014), "the hand of Allah" (048:010), (038:075) & (039:067)

Now some people may claim that these references are metaphorical, but isn't that a human projection on the word of God? Aren't we imposing our interpretation on the self-evident statements of scriptures? Further, even if we grant that such references are metaphorical, why would the scriptures repeatedly and consistently present God as having a humanlike form if in reality he didn't have one? Wouldn't that be a dangerous and misleading metaphor? Instead of audaciously claiming that the scriptures are presenting a misleading metaphor, isn't it humbler, safer and more logical to infer that it is our preconceptions that are mistaken, that are in need of correction by the words of scripture?

Further, there is the classic and clear statement in the Bible: "Man is made in the image of God." (*Ezekiel* 1:27) In which scripture is it said that God is made in the image of man? None.

The Vedic scriptures like the philosophical and devotional masterpiece Shrimad Bhagavatam reiterate and expand the understanding that God's form is the prototype on which our form is made. They reveal God's form as a bluish-black, cowherd boy, adorned with a peacock feat her, playing a flute. When our hearts are attracted to Krishna's form, then we will no longer be tormented by insatiable attractions to the temporarily-good-looking forms of this world, but will become fully satisfied by relishing Krishna's everlasting beauty. To initiate our re-attraction to him, Krishna manifests himself as the Deity.

So the correct understanding is that, far from the Deity being anthropomorphic, it is our form that is theomorphic (made according to God's form).

෮

HOW ARE THE VEDAS SPECIAL?

Question: Among the scriptures of the great religions, are the Vedic scriptures special in any way?

Answer: Let's consider three objective criteria to evaluate the contributions of the Vedic scriptures to world theology:

1. **Knowledge of God's greatness:** The scriptures of all the great religions declare that God is great. But the Vedic scriptures alone demonstrate that divine greatness in graphic details. For example, various scriptures contain statements to the effect that God contains the whole creation in him, but the Bhagavad-gita alone demonstrates this truth. In its eleventh chapter Krishna displays to Arjuna his universal form, which is one of the greatest mystical visions in world literature. Arjuna saw within the universal form—within Krishna—everything and everyone in existence: the planets, stars and universes as well as all living beings –celestial, terrestrial and sub-terrestrial.

2. **Reconciliation of God's contradictory attributes:** Most religious scriptures contain many apparently contradictory statements like God has form and God doesn't have a form, or God is transcendent to nature and God is immanent in nature. The Vedic scriptures alone resolve these contradictions by revealing a profound tripartite ontology of God's existential greatness. The quintessential Vedic text, the Srimad Bhagavatam (1.2.11), explains that God manifests as three simultaneous, non-dual manifestations:

   a. **Brahman**: The dazzling white effulgence that pervades all existence.

b. **Paramatma**: The immanent personal expansion of God who resides in the heart of every living being and in every atom.

c. **Bhagavan**: The all-attractive Supreme Person who resides in his own abode in the transcendental world.

3. **Revelation of God's love-play (lila):** Most scriptures portray God primarily as a judge who rewards the pious and penalizes the impious. If that's all God had to do eternally, even by earthly standards, his life would be quite boring. But the Srimad Bhagavatam explains that being a judge is only a tiny part of God's multifaceted, nay omni-faceted, personality. Some non-Vedic scriptures do mention that God is a God of love, but only the Vedic scriptures demonstrate this. They explain that God, in his highest abode, manifests as the supremely loving and lovable person, Krishna. To facilitate the reciprocation of pure love, Krishna, plays the role of a mischievous child and engages other devotees to play the role of being his parents, relatives and friends. This play or *lila* is not false like a drama enacted on a stage, but is the eternal, topmost reality; therein is fulfilled the most real of all our longings: to love and  to be loved. The concept of *lila* is the unique contribution of the Vedic scriptures to world theology and it has the potential to evoke unmatched divine love among those devoted to God.

Understanding the specialty of the Vedic revelation using these objective criteria shouldn't make us arrogant, but should make us responsible to develop genuine love for God and share it with the world.

ॐ

WHY CONTRADICTIONS IN SCRIPTURES?

Question: The Vedic texts give contradictory descriptions of God by stating that he has form and that he has no form. Are these contradictions reconcilable?

Answer: Let's consider a verse from the *Shvetashvatara Upanishad* (3.19)

> *apani-pado javano grahita pashyaty acakshuh sa shrinoty akarnah*

This verse contains an apparent contradiction: pashyaty acaksuh "God has no eyes, but he sees." How is this contradiction to be reconciled?

The Vedic tradition contains a special *pramana* (method of acquiring knowledge) called *arthapatti* (postulation) that is used for reconciling contradictory statements. *Arthapatti* involves postulating a third statement that reconciles the two statements. To see how *arthapatti* works, consider the two contradictory statements:

1. Ravi does not eat food during the day 2. Ravi is growing fat	The *arthapatti* to reconcile these two statements would be: Ravi eats in the night.

Similarly, the *arthapatti* to reconcile the statements about God having and not having a form is: God has no material form, but has a spiritual form.

Question: Why do the Vedic scriptures contain such contradictory statements at all? Wouldn't it be much better if they gave truths clearly and unambiguously?

Answer: The seemingly contradictory descriptions serve the vital purpose of challenging our preconceptions and stimulating us to rise to a higher understanding.

Consider the following *Ishopanishad* verse (mantra 8):

sa paryagac chukram akayam avranam
ashnaviram shuddham apapa-viddham

This verse describes God as akayam (having no body) and then as ashnaviram (having no veins). If God has no body, why is there a need to describe that he has no veins? Isn't it obvious that someone who has no body has no veins? The Ishopanishad wants us to rise to the higher understanding that God has a special kind of body that has no veins.

God is described as *akayam* because the word *kaya* (body) has several connotations that do not apply to God. A body is that which:

1. Is separate from the real person, the soul
2. Is a product of the past karma of the soul
3. Tends to degrade the soul by stimulating bodily desires
4. Has to be given up in due course of time

None of these apply to the Lord, whose body and soul are nondifferent, who has no karmic past, who is never degraded and whose body is eternal. Because we tend to superimpose our material conceptions on God, the scriptures sometimes use negative words like *akayam* to emphasize that God does not have any body – like ours. Why is it important to understand the difference between our material form and God's spiritual form? Material forms are temporary, so attraction to them leads only to eventual frustration. But God's form is eternal, so attraction to his form leads to ultimate fulfillment. The negative scriptural statements that God doesn't have a form (like ours) save us from the frustration and the positive scriptural statements lead us to the fulfillment.

৪৩

IS THE IDOL GOD?

Question: Some people consider the temple *murti* (idol) to be a symbol of God, while others consider it to be God himself. What is the correct understanding?

Answer: The *murti* is God himself.

To understand how, let's analyze the two kinds of symbolism: ascending and descending. Ascending symbolism involves ascribing a concrete or tangible symbol to an abstract or amorphous concept. For example, the flag of a nation is the ascending symbol for the concept of nationhood. In ascending symbolism, the only connection between the symbol (flag) and the concept (nationhood) is the connection imagined in the minds of those adopting that symbol. Such symbolism is used because the concrete symbol (flag) evokes feelings (patriotism) better than the abstract concept (nationhood). That's why, if a new flag better evokes patriotism, the old flag is discarded. Some people conceive the *murti* similarly: "I like this form of God and so I will worship it; if you like some other form, you can worship that. And if I start liking another form tomorrow, I will worship that form."

However, this notion is incorrect.

Why? Because it assumes that God is abstract and amorphous, and so can be ascribed any symbol by one's ascending imagination. But that assumption itself is wrong. The Vedic scriptures declare that God is a person with a specific, concrete form and that He personally descends as the *murti*, more aptly called as the Deity.

The Deity is thus an example of descending symbolism. To understand this type of symbolism, consider the example of a photo given by the philosopher-saint Bhaktivinoda Thakura. When we see the photo of a loved one, that photo depicts the actual form of our beloved. So, the photo evokes our affection for that specific person, not for some abstract concept. The same principle applies to the Deity, for the Deity, when made according 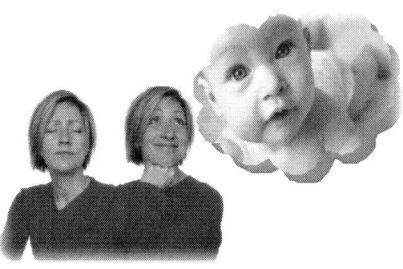 to the scriptural descriptions of God's form, precisely depicts that divine form.

In fact, there's much more to a Deity than a photo. When we look lovingly at the photo, that person is not present in the photo to reciprocate. But when the great devotees of God lovingly behold and serve the Deity, to reciprocate with their love, God descends from the spiritual realm into the material arena as the Deity. That's why devotees with pure love can see and experience the Deity to be nondifferent from God. To the extent we lack such love, to that extent the Deity will seem a mere symbol of God. But if we serve the Deity with the desire to develop pure love, then, the more our love will develop, the more our realization will ascend and gradually we will realize that the Deity is not a symbol of God, but is God himself.

(A detailed analysis of this subject is offered in the author's book *Idol Worship or Ideal Worship?*)

☙

WHY CAN'T GOD PROTECT HIMSELF?

Question: If the Deity (*murti*) is non-different from God, then how can a fly move around the Deity and the Deity doesn't – or can't – wave it away?

Answer: When God manifests himself through any material  manifestation, the divinity of that manifestation is demonstrated not by its potency to break material laws, but by its potency to bring about spiritual transformation among the sincerely devoted. For example, some religions which don't accept the practice of Deity worship still worship their sacred texts as if they were divine. Yet can those sacred texts not be torn or burnt by the faithless? Obviously, they can be. But does this make them any less divine? Not at all. The divinity of these texts cannot be experienced by defiantly tearing them apart to check whether they miraculously save themselves; their divinity can be experienced only by reading them with a devotional service attitude. The same principle applies to the Deity.

Can the Deity not wave away the fly? He can, but he doesn't. Why? Because the Lord does not manifest himself as the Deity to prove his omnipotence. In fact, the Lord generally does not manifest his omnipotence in this material world. Why? Because this world is provided as a facility for those souls who want to enjoy separate from God. All of us were originally with God in his eternal spiritual kingdom, but when we wanted to enjoy by imitating him instead of serving him, then we exiled ourselves to this material world to play out our fantasies of becoming the best, or, in other words, becoming

God. But God is eternally the supreme, the best in everything. If He were to manifest his omnipotence in this word, then nobody would have any chance to even try to play God. So, God graciously facilitates our desire to enjoy separate from him by not directly manifesting his omnipotence here.

He wants us to realize for ourselves that, no matter how big and powerful we become, we can never be happy without loving him. So, as soon as we get the slightest desire to turn back to him, He starts providing us facilities to love him again. One of the most important of such facilities is the Deity. The Deity offers us what no other divine manifestation does: the opportunity to serve God personally by beholding, bowing down, praying, touching, bathing, dressing, decorating and offering food.

Knowing thus that the Deity is a special mercy manifestation of God, how should we respond on seeing a fly near the Deity on the altar? Philosophically, we should understand that the Deity has allowed the fly there to graphically show how we are neglecting our service to the Deity, how we are not keeping the altar clean. Practically, we should hasten to remove the fly and make arrangements by which flies will not disturb the Deity again.

ॐ

WHY BUILD TEMPLES?

Question: Why does ISKCON build huge temples? What do temples contribute to society?

Answer: Just as food, clothing and shelter are the basic needs of the  body, peace is a basic need of the mind. Today's society offers very little facility to provide this basic mental need. Instead, our fast-paced, stress-filled lifestyle does a lot to take away our peace of mind. No wonder the WHO declared that the greatest medical challenge of the current century is not AIDS or cancer, but mental health problems.

Peace of mind is not a luxury, but a necessity that creates the foundation for us to effectively execute our duties. If we have to lift a 5 kg bag for a few minutes, that's not difficult. But if we have to lift it continuously for the rest of our lives, it will soon become an unbearable burden. Only if we if take periodic breaks that allow our muscles to rest and regain strength can we lift the weight lifelong. Similarly, our duties – and the anxieties that they inevitably cause – are like burdens on our minds. If we let these anxieties weigh on our minds constantly, they will drain our mental energy and may even cause a mental breakdown. The temple is a place where we can take off that mental burden and refresh our minds with the healing serenity that pervades the temple. Thus a temple provides an essential service for the community, a service that is provided by very few other places.

Of course, not all temples are equally potent. The more the divine vibrations that pervade a temple, the greater the tranquility that we can experience there. Thos e vibrations result from:

1. The presence and worship of the Lord in His deity form

2. The constant chanting of His holy names

3. The broadcasting of His empowering message, as taught in the sacred scriptures

4. The association of saintly personalities who share God's love with one and all

At many ISKCON temples throughout the world, hundreds of people come every evening to de-stress themselves after a hard day's work. They take darshan of the deities, attend the arti and take in the divine atmosphere. Thus mentally rested and recharged, they resume their duties with greater effectiveness.

Those who unfortunately don't take such breaks become confused or lethargic in their personal functioning and irritable or overwhelmed in their interpersonal dealings, leading to many avoidable problems. That's why Srila Prabhupada, wanted to have temples right in the heart of the city so that maximum number of people would have easy, quick access to the tranquility that the temple offers.

(For a detailed answer to this question, please refer to the author's pocket book *Why do we Need a Temple?*)

℘

CAN DANCE AND MEDITATION UNITE?

Question: Shouldn't meditation be silent and sober? How can dancing kirtans be called a form of meditation?

Answer: *Sankirtana*, the congregational chanting of the holy names of Krishna to the accompaniment of music and dance, is actually meditation in its most profound, potent and practical form. Let's see how.

The purpose of meditation is to connect with and experience spiritual reality. Silent meditation, as done through breathing exercises and yogic postures, tries to achieve this by negating the material, by deactivating the body and the mind. But since we're habituated to physical and mental activity, wouldn't it be easier and more natural if somehow the body and the mind could be used to raise ourselves to spiritual levels of consciousness? That is precisely what *sankirtana* does. Engaging the body in graceful dance for the pleasure of the Lord, and the mind in prayerful contemplation on the sound of His holy names—especially the maha-mantra: Hare Krishna, Hare Krishna, Krishna Krishna, Hare Hare / Hare Rama, Hare Rama, Rama Rama, Hare Hare—quickly and efficaciously transports our consciousness to the joyful realm of divine love.

Sankirtana acts like spiritual-music therapy to heal the soul in the current Iron Age, Kali-yuga. Just as a stone burdens the person carrying it, negative thoughts and emotions burden most people in the present age. *Sankirtana* floods the heart with positive, uplifting emotions like love, faith and joy and flushes away negative, burdensome emotions like hatred, anxiety and sorrow.

Shri Chaitanya Mahaprabhu, who appeared some five hundred years ago, revived and popularized *sankirtana* all over India.

Lord Chaitanya displayed divine dance so enchantingly that His golden complexion, graceful gait, and intense devotional emotions charmed everyone—from aristocrats like the king of Orissa down to crime-hardened rogues.

Indeed, Shri Chaitanya's dance charmed even the Muslim emperor Akbar, who lived half a century later: "Hail Thee, O Chaitanya, the victor of my heart.... O my heart's Lord, how can I express the love I have for Thee? Shah Akbar craves a drop from the sea of Thy love and piety." (Quoted by D. C. Sen in *Chaitanya and His Age*) These verses composed by a Muslim emperor in glorification of one who is commonly considered a Hindu saint illustrate the universal appeal of this dancing meditation.

As a spiritual master in Chaitanya Mahaprabhu's line, Srila Prabhupada, through his ISKCON, popularized the divine dance of *sankirtana* in our times. Chanting and dancing devotees are now a familiar sight in major cities all over the world. Given that dance, an exuberant physical activity, and meditation, an introspective spiritual activity, intersect in *sankirtana*, it can well be called the ultimate dance.

YOGA OF LOVE?

Question: Is there any relationship between yoga and love?

Answer: Certainly; there is a deep relationship.

Yoga, with its extraordinary health benefits, has achieved global acclaim today. The word 'yoga' comes  from the root 'yug', which is similar to the English word 'yoke' and means to 'connect' or 'link'. The *Patanjali Yoga-Sutra*, which is the foundational guidebook for yoga, explains that yoga in its completeness comprises eight stages and so is called *ashtanga-yoga* (*ashta* – eight, *anga* - limbs). What is popular as yoga today is actually just one of the eight stages named asana. The *Yoga-Sutra* also states that the final stage of yoga is called *samadhi*: loving, trancelike absorption on the Lord in the heart.

The ancient Vedic wisdom-tradition that gave us the *Yoga-Sutra* reminds us that yoga can offer gifts far greater than healing the body or even calming the mind. In its most evolved form, yoga can fulfill our innermost need: love.

More than treasures and pleasures, positions and possessions, our deepest longing is for love; all of us want to love and to be loved. Nowadays, love is often reduced to the bodily interaction between people. But real love is a connection beyond bodies, beyond minds, beyond even the souls. True love enables us to connect with others at an eternal dimension by centering our relationship on the origin of all love: the all-attractive, all-loving Lord.

This art of centering and connecting our love is called bhakti. It is the universal wisdom that underlies and unifies all the great wisdom-traditions of the world. Bhakti empowers us to tune our consciousness so that we can receive love from the Lord who is at the heart of the creation and then radiate that love to all whom we contact, thus enriching many, many love-starved hearts with warmth and joy. No wonder then that bhakti is called the yoga of love.

As bhakti take us most efficaciously to samadhi, the ultimate stage of yoga, Lord Krishna in the *Bhagavad-gita* (6.47) states explicitly that bhakti-yoga is the topmost all yogas: "Of all yogis, the one with great faith who always abides in me, thinks of me within himself, and renders transcendental loving service to me is the most intimately united with me in yoga and is the highest of all."

The Lord is so eager to satisfy our hunger for love that he makes himself fully available to us as his holy names – especially the chant of love, the Hare Krishna mahamantra. When we devotionally chant the holy names, we are simultaneously linking with God (yoga), and are also expressing our love for God and exeriencing his love for us. Thus, by linking the love-seeking soul with the love-radiating Supersoul, chanting constitutes the pinnacle of the yoga of love.

WHY THE CASTE SYSTEM?

Question: The caste system has led to so much discrimination and exploitation in Indian society. Why was such a division given in the Vedic literature?

Answer: Firstly, the present caste system, in which the caste is  determined by birth, is not given in the Vedic literature. The original name for the Vedic social division of labor was *varnashrama*. The *Bhagavad-gita* (4.13) declares that the system of *varnashrama* is based on *guna* (qualities) and *karma* (activities) or, in modern parlance, attitudes and aptitudes – not on birth.

Secondly, what causes discrimination? Almost always materialism, which makes people imagine that material things – wealth and comforts, power and prestige, positions and  possessions – are the only way to happiness. As we live in a world of limited resources and unlimited wants, plenty for one causes scarcity for another. When the powerful become materialistic, they encroach upon the quota of the weak, leading to social inequities. The antidote for materialism is spirituality, which provides inner fulfillment and cures the exploitative mentality. And *varnashrama* was the best social order not only to foster spiritual enlightenment and experience, but also to have optimal social utilization of individual abilities. The biased imperial propaganda during the British rule has blinded us Indians to what is good in our own culture, as pointed out by Mark Tully, BBC correspondent for India: "The alienation of many young people in the West and the loneliness of the old show the suffering that egalitarianism inflicts on those who do not win, the superficiality of an egalitarianism which in effect means equal opportunities for all to win and then ignores the inevitable losers. For all that, the elite of India have become so spellbound by egalitarianism that they are unable to see any good in the only institution which does provide a sense of identity and dignity to those who are robbed from birth of the opportunity to compete on an equal footing: caste."

In his book *Man, the Master*, researcher Gerald Heard glorifies the traditional Indian social division as "organic democracy", as "the rule of the people who have organized themselves in a living and not a mechanical relationship; where instead of all men being said to be equal, which is a lie, all men are known to be of equal value, could we but find the position in which their potential  contribution could be released and their essential growth so pursued."

As modern intelligent Indians, we should certainly do all that we can to end caste discrimination. At the same time, while striving to remove the cataract of casteism, let us make sure that we don't pluck out the eye of Vedic spiritual wisdom. Rather, by understanding and applying those spiritual teachings, we can show the world the way to a lasting unity based on genuine spirituality.

(For a detailed answer to this question, please refer to the article "Caste System – Material Diversity, Spiritual Equality" in the author's book *Science and Spirituality*)

શ

DOES RELIGION CAUSE WAR?

Question: Religion causes wars. Wouldn't the world be much better off without religion?

Answer: Let's discuss the answer in four points:

1. How many of the wars in recent memory were caused by  religion? Religion was not an issue in either of the two world wars, nor in most of the other wars like the Vietnam War or the Korean War. Even when religion has been supposedly involved, the amount of religious warfare has been far less than the amount of secular warfare (warfare motivated by secular causes like money, power, politics, prestige etc).

2. Even when religion is the professed cause, is it the actual cause? Terrorists, mercenaries, suicide bombers and soldiers who engage in violence in the name of religion are promised materialistic rewards: wealth that their family members and relatives will get in this world. But non-religious people also engage in similar violence for material gains. The so-called religious people engaging in violence are motivated not by religion, but by materialism; religion merely serves as their self-righteous rationalization.

3. Even if religion has been misused, is giving up religion the solution? Scientific technology has also been misused to wreak unspeakable suffering through the weapons of mass destruction. If we were to give up whatever is misused, we would have to give up technology. If there is a cataract in the eye, we need to remove not the eye, but the cataract. Similarly,

we need to remove not religion, but the ignorance of true religion that lets vested interest abuse religion. The number of people who are inspired to acts of service and compassion by religion is far, far more than the number of people incited to violence by it. By highlighting the violent acts  perpetrated in the name of religion and by downplaying the charitable acts performed due to religious inspiration, our media gives a misleading picture of the contribution of religion to the world.

4. Real spirituality – which comprises of philosophy and religion – enables us to attain inner happiness, which is the prerequisite for peace. We are all souls, who are the lost children of God, Krishna. Due to not finding inner happiness, we have become filled with desires for external enjoyment and are forced to fight with each other for the scarce resources necessary to fulfill our desires. So, as long as we seek happiness externally, we cannot end wars. And the best, nay the only, way to find inner happiness is through genuine spirituality comprised of philosophical understanding and religious practice.

Thus, real religion does not cause wars; it ends wars.

(For a detailed answer, please refer to the article "Does Religion Cause War?" in the author's book *Science and Spirituality*)

౸

CONVERTER! CONVERT YOURSELF!

Question: Some religionists are converting people to their religion by offering financial benefits for converting. What is the Vedic perspective on this?

Answer: It is a sad fact that today most religions have become highly superficial and commercialized, with overzealous missionaries imagining that God is their exclusive monopoly and that His grace is their patented product. Often, due to such superficial spiritual realization, their sense of security and success comes not from their internal devotion to God, but from their external ability to get more and more people to accept their path as the only right path. So, they offer allurements to convert people to their religion and thus boost their internal security and external political strength. Real spiritual advancement takes place only when people are converted vertically from being materialists to becoming spiritualists, from

 being devoted to worldly things to becoming devoted to God. But when people convert for material gains, such conversion is mostly horizontal. Before conversion, they were materialists belonging to one religion; after conversion, they continue to remain materialists, with just their religious label changed. Such conversion from one brand of materialism to another does no spiritual good either to the converter or the converted. In fact, it often does harm by inducing feelings of hatred among the converts toward their earlier religion, and thus disrupting the social harmony in the family and the

community

In marked contrast with such superficial converters are deep religionists who take inspiration from sincere followers of others paths. Srila Bhaktivinoda Thakura, a nineteenth century Vaishnava saint-scholar expresses this broad-minded spirit: "When we have occasion to be present at the place of worship of other religionists at the time of their worship, we should stay there in a respectful mood, contemplating thus: 'Here is  being worshiped my adorable highest entity God, in a different form than that of mine. Due to a different practice of a different kind, I cannot thoroughly comprehend this system of theirs. But seeing it, I am feeling a greater attachment for my own system. God is one. I bow down before His emblem as I see here and offer my prayer to my Lord who has adopted this different emblem so that He may increase my love toward Him in the form that is acceptable for me'."

Today, people are being increasingly plundered of their wealth of inner happiness by the common enemy of all religions: atheistic materialism. So people do need conversion, a vertical conversion that empowers them to find internal happiness by substantially increasing their devotion and dedication to God. Therefore, all religionists need to look inward first to understand and practice the deep spiritual essence of their religious tradition. When they have thus converted themselves, then, if they look outward to share that essence with others, they can do true good to themselves and to the world.

ॐ

SAVED FROM "SAVIORS"?

Question: Religious sermonizers talk of loving and saving everyone, but often foster hatred toward those who don't follow their path. Why is that?

Answer: Because the people fostering such hatred are not truly religious. Many people have a primitive, tribal "we-they" mindset. They see existence as a perpetual battle between "we" versus "they", where "they" refers to their competitors or enemies. When religious zeal becomes superimposed on this tribal mentality, then the battle takes the form of "the good we" versus "the evil they", where "they" includes all those who don't follow "our true religion". Once religious conflict gets rationalized as a battle against evil, then religionists become blinded to their own evil deeds, for they feel their "noble" ends justify any means, no matter how evil.

However, this unfortunate situation arises only when the religion is not based on sound philosophy. Therefore, the Vedic scriptures provide a profound and practical philosophy that can raise people from this tribal mentality to universal consciousness. They state that all living beings are the beloved children of one God and so, spiritually, we are all one family, as celebrated in the famous Vedic aphorism *vasudhaiva kutumbakam*.  People are categorized as good or evil, not by their religious label, but by rational, objective parameters, viz., their qualities. The Bhagavad-gita analyzes all material existence in terms of the three modes of material nature: goodness (*sattva-guna*), passion (*rajo-guna*) and ignorance (*tamo-guna*). The modes are subtle, psychic forces that shape the interaction between consciousness and matter. Those affected by goodness are characterized by knowledge, thoughtfulness and satisfaction; those affected by passion are characterized by cravings for pleasure, power and prestige; and those affected by ignorance are characterized by laziness, intoxication and violence. Beyond goodness is transcendence,

which bestows the enlightened vision to practically see the loving relationship among all living beings. The more people are infected by passion and ignorance, the more they tend to evil. The more they are permeated by goodness and transcendence, the more they gravitate to good.

All people – including even religious people – are infected by the modes and are accordingly good or evil to varying degrees. Various religions are essentially like different hospitals meant to cure people of their infection. Just as patients don't get cured merely by entering into a hospital, religionists don't get "saved" just by stamping themselves as belonging to a particular religion. They will be saved only when they diligently practice their religious disciplines like prayer, worship, and meditation, and change their qualities. Unfortunately, not understanding or practicing the essence of their own religion, superficial religionists imagine that other religionists are evil, when they themselves are gripped by evil qualities.

May the Lord save the world from being "saved" by them!

AN INDIAN INDIA?

Question: How can India benefit from modernization without losing her culture to westernization?

Answer: To modernize India without westernizing her, it's vital that Indians understand the glory of the Vedic literature that lies at the foundation of Indian culture. As many Indians are enamored by the West, let's consider a few among the many quotes of Western scholars who have lavishly appreciated the Vedic culture and literature.

The German philosopher Johann Gottfried von Herder stated, "The Brahmins (the spiritual intelligentsia of India) have wonderful wisdom and strength to form their people in great degrees of gentleness, courtesy, temperance, and chastity. They have so effectively established their people in these virtues that in comparison, Europeans frequently appear as beastly, drunken or mad." Another famous German philosopher, Arthur Schopenhauer declared the Upanishads to be "the production of the highest human wisdom" and proclaimed, "It is the most satisfying and elevated reading which is possible in the world; it has been my solace in life and will be the solace of my death." Frenchman Voltaire, the quintessential Enlightenment thinker, asserted, "I am convinced that everything has come down to us from the banks of the Ganges: astronomy, astrology, metempsychosis, etc." The French historian Jules Michelet felt certain that India was "the womb of the world."

These scholars lived before the British gained political control over India. Once colonial interests took over, subsequent scholars were paid and engaged to systematically denigrate and misinterpret the Vedic literature so that Indians would voluntarily become westernized and Christianized. Even after independence, the neglect of the Vedic literature continued because most of independent India's leaders, though politically free, remained cultural slaves of the West.

But thankfully for India, she still had visionary spiritual leaders like Srila Prabhupada. By inspiring millions of people all over the world to adopt Vedic culture, Srila Prabhupada inspired generations of westernized Indians to return to their own culture. Srila Prabhupada envisioned an East-West synthesis; spreading Indian spiritual wisdom with Western material technology. He compared the coming together of Vedic spirituality and modern technology to the coming together of the proverbial blind man and the lame man. His vision has materialized in ISKCON, where sophisticated laser shows offer breathtaking darshans of Krishna and state-of-the-art animatronics exhibitions depict the Bhagavad-gita dialogue between Krishna and Arjuna. Aren't these living, stunning examples of modernization without westernization? The more we Indians study, understand and apply the principles given in the Vedic literature, the more we will discover for themselves the extraordinary internal satisfaction that comes thereof. When a significant number of us choose to thus spiritually enrich ourselves, then we can usher in a modern yet Indian India.

A Special Note to the Reader

Dear Reader,

I hope your investment of time in reading this book yielded the return of intellectual enrichment. I would love to hear from you about your comments, suggestions, critiques and questions. I will try my best to personally respond to every one of your correspondences. If your questions have a universal appeal, I will try to include the articles that answer them in the future volumes of this FAQ series.

I await your correspondence at faqbook@voicepune.com or 4, Tarapore Road, Next to Dastur Boys' School, Camp, Pune - 411001.

If you would like to continue the learning stimulated by this book, then here a couple of books I wholeheartedly recommend:

- For a systematic study of the wide variety of topics covered in this book, the *Essence of Bhagavad-gita* series by Radheshyam Das, Director, VOICE, Pune offers an excellent, contemporary presentation.

- For a verse-by-verse translation and commentary on the *Bhagavad-gita* (the book that is the basis of most of the answers in this book), the *Bhagavad Gita As It Is* by A C Bhaktivedanta Swami Srila Prabhupada is the globally-acclaimed classic that is the most widely read English rendition of the Gita.

With best wishes for your journey to life's ultimate destination,

Chaitanya Charan das

Acknowledgements

The first and foremost acknowledgements for this book are due to HG Radheshyam Prabhu, my spiritual mentor and publisher, whose selfless and tireless dedication is an enduring inspiration.

I thank my beloved spiritual master, His Holiness Radhanath Maharaj, whose actions and words are the compass according to which I aspire to orient my writing and my life.

His Holiness Jayadvaita Maharaj, my "writing guru", is world-famous for his precise and penetrating answers to questions. I hope this book written in a QA format following his inimitable example will please him.

My very special thanks are due to my dear godbrother, Padmalochan Prabhu, for his creativity in designing the innovative cover page, patience in tolerating my repeated editing and dedication in scrupulously formatting the whole book.

Manish V, resourceful as ever, offer insightful suggestions, especially for the article and book titles.

Navadvipa Pati Prabhu has consistently helped in formatting the individual articles. Shyamalila Prabhu and his team helped with the pictures, as did Purushottam K.

Sagar M has been a research assistant of unparalleled resourcefulness and promptness.

Praveen S battled against poor health and tight schedules to help with proofreading, in which he was ably assisted by Aditya HK.

Venkata B repeatedly and insistently suggested the idea of compiling the articles into a book and kindly supported the publication.

Many others including Sripad Mahaprabhu P, Kiran C, Abhijit T and Swaminathan N helped in ways that perhaps only a writer can understand.

My heartfelt thanks to them all.

And last, but not the least, i thank all of you, my readers. This book resulted because many intelligent and inquisitive readers like you asked questions.

Chaitanya Charan Das

BOOKS PUBLISHED BY VOICE

Essence of Bhagavad-gita (EBG) series:
- EBG Course-1: 'Spritual Scientist'
- EBG Coursc-2: 'Positive Thinker'
- EBG Course-3: 'Self Manager'
- EBG Course-4: 'Proactive Leader'
- EBG Course-5: 'Personality Development'
- EBG Vol -1 of 2 (Marathi)
- EBG Vol -1 of 2 (Hindi)

Spirituality for the Modern Youth series
- Discover Yourself
- Your Best Friend
- Your Secret Journey
- Victory Over Death
- Yoga of Love

Pocket Books
- How to Harness Mind Power?
- Practical Tips to Mind Control
- Can I Live Forever?
- Do We Live More Than Once?
- Misdirected Love
- E.N.E.R.G.Y- Your sutra for Positive Thinking
- Recession- Adversity or Opportunity?
- Why do we need a T.E.M.P.L.E?

Other Books
- Youth Preaching Manual
- Bhagavad-gita 7 Day Course
- Values
- Frequently Un-Answered Questions

- Spiritual Scientist Vol I and II (Selected Newspaper articles)
- Science and Spirituality

Children's Books:

- My First Krishna Book
- Getting to Know Krishna
- More About Krishna
- Deovtees of Krishna
- Wonderful Krishna
- Krishna's Childhood Pastimes
- Janmashtami
- Krishna Colors

Bring out the LEADER in you series

These books will be suitable for college students as well as corporates. The first book in this series has been published and the remaining will be released in the near future.

1. Stress Management
2. Time Management
3. Art of Self Management
4. Power of Habits
5. Secret of Concentration
6. Mind Your Mind
7. Positive Mental Attitude
8. Team Playing & Winning Trust of Others
9. Overcoming Inferiority Complex
10. Constructive Criticism – How to Give It or Take It?
11. Fate and Free Will
12. Karma – The Law of Infallible Justice
13. Key to Real Happiness
14. Conflict Resolution
15. Eight Qualities of an Effective Leader

16. Managing Our Anger
17. Self Development
18. Personality Development and Character Buildup
19. Proactive Leadership
20. Art of Living and Leaving

For details about **VOICE books**, please contact:
Krishna Kishore Das, Sales Manager,
4, Tarapore Road, Pune Camp, Pune-1,
E-mail: voicebooks@voicepune.com,
       krishnakishoredas@gmail.com
Ph: +91-20-41033222 (Ext. 219), +91-9822451260

VOICE also offers various **Certificate Courses**
For details please contact:
Corporate VOICE,
4, Tarapore Road, Pune Camp, Pune-1,
E-mail: corporatevoice@voicepune.com,
Ph: +91-20-41033222 (Ext. 227)

For FREE subscription of our weekly cyber magazine
"The Spiritual Scientist"
please enroll at **www.thespiritualscientist.com**

Made in United States
North Haven, CT
26 May 2023

37014336R00072